GETTING STARTED WITH
Electronics

by Cathleen Shamieh

WILEY

GETTING STARTED WITH ELECTRONICS

Published by
John Wiley & Sons, Inc.
111 River Street
Hoboken, NJ 07030-5774

www.wiley.com

For general information on our other products and services, please contact our Customer Care Department within the U.S. at 877-762-2974, outside the U.S. at 317-572-3993, or fax 317-572-4002. For technical support, please visit https://hub.www.wiley.com/community/support/dummies.

Wiley publishes in a variety of print and electronic formats and by print-on-demand. Some material included with standard print versions of this book may not be included in e-books or in print-on-demand. If this book refers to media such as a CD or DVD that is not included in the version you purchased, you may download this material at http://booksupport.wiley.com. For more information about Wiley products, visit www.wiley.com.

Library of Congress Control Number: 2016947892

ISBN 978-1-119-31380-9 (pbk); 978-1-119-31382-3 (epdf); 978-1-119-31381-6 (epub)

Manufactured in the United States of America

10 9 8 7 6 5 4 3 2 1

CONTENTS

ITRODUCTION

GREETINGS, FUTURE ENGINEERS!

Welcome to *Getting Started with Electronics* — the book that gives you a jump-start into the exciting world of electronics.

Electronics is all about controlling *electrical current* — which you may know better as electricity — flowing in a complete path called a *circuit*. All electronic devices are made up of circuits, and every circuit contains a power supply, a path, and one or more parts (known as *electronic components*) to control current flow.

ABOUT THIS BOOK

Getting Started with Electronics walks you through six electronics projects you can build and show off to your family and friends. Each project includes a list of the parts you need, step-by-step circuit-building instructions, and loads of colorful illustrations to guide you.

By completing all the projects in this book, you will

» Discover how to build a complete circuit

» Build circuits on a breadboard

» Light an LED — without frying it

» Switch electrical current between paths

» Control sound using light

» Use an integrated circuit (IC) to control lights and sound

» Pull a radio signal out of thin air and listen to it

After reading this book, you'll have enough knowledge and experience to join Apple as a circuit designer for the next-generation iPhone.

Just kidding! (You didn't really believe me, did you?)

Okay, so I can't promise that this book will get you a job in electronics, but I will promise that you'll have fun building circuits — and that you'll learn a bit about electronics along the way.

ABOUT YOU

In writing this book, I made a few assumptions about you and other readers:

» You don't know much — if anything — about electronics.

» You're interested in fun circuits that are easy to build.

» You have some money to spend on supplies and tools. With some smart shopping, $20 will get you most of what you need and $70 to $100 will cover everything.

» You're able to place an online order for electronic components and get to a store or two (with help from an adult).

» You will carefully follow the safety tips in this book.

ABOUT THE ICONS

The tip icon flags time-saving shortcuts and other information that can make your circuit-building job easier.

This icon alerts you to important ideas or facts that you should keep in mind while building your electronics projects.

When you build electronic circuits, you're bound to run into situations that call for extreme caution. The warning icon reminds you to take extra care to avoid injury or prevent damage to your components or circuits.

UPDATES

Nobody's perfect, least of all me. In the event that someone (whether it be me, an editor, or a reader) discovers an error (or two or more) in this book, I will provide updates at www.dummies.com. Search for *Getting Started with Electronics* and then open the Download tab on this book's dedicated page.

THE FIRST STEP

Getting Started with Electronics isn't like a typical novel that you read from start to finish. It's more like a book of short stories or, in this case, projects. It's perfectly fine to pick a project that interests you and build it — even if you haven't built the earlier projects in the book.

But if you choose to jump into a later project first, you'd be smart to read Project 1 before you get started. Project 1 lists everything you need to build the projects in the book and walks you step-by-step through the shopping process to ensure that it's as easy, quick, and inexpensive as possible.

No matter how you choose to use *Getting Started with Electronics*, I hope you have a lot of fun building the projects in this book!

PROJECT 1 SHOPPING SPREE

DO YOU LIKE TO SHOP? (I DON'T!)

To build the projects in this book, you need to buy a bunch of *electronic components* (including resistors, capacitors, diodes, LEDs, transistors, a speaker, an earphone, and an integrated circuit), accessories (such as alligator clips and wires), tools (such as wire strippers), and other supplies.

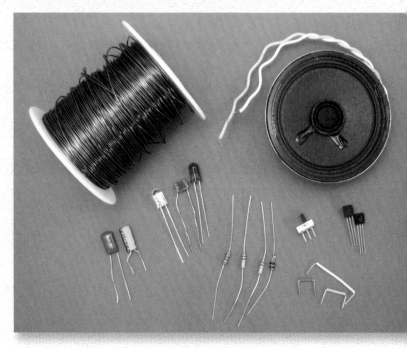

PLAN YOUR SHOPPING SPREE

I wish I could name a store in a shopping mall close to your house where you could just walk in, pick out all the parts you need, plunk down about $50, and go home and start building projects. Unfortunately, there is no such store (even RadioShack stores no longer carry a wide variety of electronic components).

So, you will need to order many of your supplies online, which means you have to plan to allow time for shipping. The good news is that you can save a lot of money by shopping online, and you can get most of the components you need in just one online trip (with an adult's assistance or, at least, an adult's credit card). You may still need to go to a couple of local stores to pick up some tools and other supplies.

Here are some recommended suppliers:

» **Tayda Electronics:** The www.TaydaElectronics.com website is easy to use (see the sidebar "How to Order Online"). One visit to Tayda and you can order nearly every electronic component and some of the accessories you need at reasonable prices (many for just pennies).

Tayda has a $5 order minimum, so try to buy everything you need in one order.

With warehouses in Colorado (US) and Bangkok (Thailand), Tayda ships worldwide. Allow 1–4 weeks for delivery, depending on where you live.

I've provided Tayda part numbers for many of the components you need in the next section.

» **Fry's Electronics:** Between its stores (in several US states) and website (www.Frys.com), Fry's stocks many of the electronic components and accessories you need. Fry's ships worldwide.

» **Farnell element14:** Start at www.Farnell.com and select your country for the Farnell element14 company in your region. (The US company is called Newark.) You'll find all the electronic components and many accessories you need.

The Farnell website is geared for adults who work in the electronics industry, so you will probably need an adult's help to make sense out of the highly technical product descriptions.

» **RadioShack:** RadioShack has stores in many parts of the US, but the stores have a limited supply of electronic components. You may find a better selection on RadioShack's online store (www.RadioShack.com). Prices are significantly higher at RadioShack than at other online suppliers, but if you really need a certain component right away (say, for instance, you burned out all your LEDs and you need just one to finish a project) and your local store has it, it's worth the trip.

You can also find most (or all) of the components, accessories, tools and supplies you need on www.Amazon.com or www.eBay.com. However, the product information is often unclear and incomplete, so be sure you know exactly what you're ordering.

Whenever you order online, make sure you understand how much the seller charges for shipping and how long it takes the seller to pack up and deliver your order.

BUDGET

If you're a smart shopper and order online, you can purchase all the electronic components and accessories you need for roughly $33 plus tax and shipping. (Of that $33, $16 is for two parts you need for Project 7, Radio.) You may spend about another $30 (plus tax) on tools and other supplies at local stores, if your family doesn't already have what you need. If you buy a lot of your components and supplies in a RadioShack store, budget another $20 or so.

If you have a limited budget, you can save money by skipping Project 7. For as little as $20 to $22, you can buy all the components you need for Projects 2-6.

HOW TO ORDER ONLINE

You might find it helpful to see exactly how to shop for electronic components from an online supplier. Let's take a look at the steps involved in ordering from Tayda Electronics:

1 In the address field of your favorite Internet browser, type the web address www.TaydaElectronics.com to bring up the home page for Tayda Electronics.

2 Locate the search field in the upper-right corner of the home page.

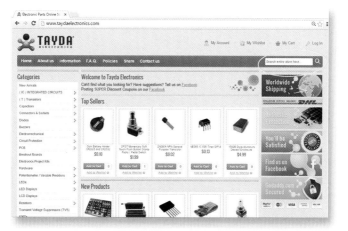

3 Type either a product code or a product name in the search field to bring up a product listing.

(continued)

(continued)

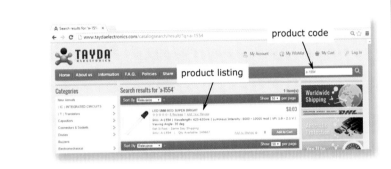

product code

product listing

4 Choose the specific product you need.

For instance, there are different types of 330-ohm resistors, but the type you need is 1/4-watt (W) carbon film.

5 Type the quantity of the product you need.

Note that some items have a minimum quantity. For instance, the resistors you need are sold in packs of ten.

product name

quantity

6 Add the item(s) to your shopping cart by clicking Add to Cart.

7 Repeat Steps 3-6 for each product you'd like to order.

You can check to see what's in your shopping cart at any time by clicking View Your Cart at the top right of your screen. Note that Tayda requires a $5 minimum order.

8 When you have selected all the products you want to order, click Proceed to Checkout, at the bottom of your shopping cart page.

(continued)

(continued)

9 Ask an adult to complete the checkout process, which requires entering a customer name, a shipping address, and payment information.

ELECTRONIC COMPONENTS AND ACCESSORIES

This section provides a complete list of the electronic components and related parts you need to complete the projects in this book. In the list that follows, I sometimes specify a product code (identified by #) and price (as of this writing, in June 2016) to give you an idea of what to look for and roughly how much you should expect to pay. Here's your shopping list of electronic parts.

» **Batteries and accessories**

» One (minimum) fresh 9-volt disposable (not rechargeable) alkaline battery ($2.50–$5.00). (I suggest you buy two.)

» One 9-volt battery clip (sometimes called a snap connector). Tayda Electronics #A-656 ($0.10), RadioShack #2700325 ($2.99), or similar.

» Wire, alligator clips, and switches

» Jumper wires (optional). Precut, prestripped solid jumper wires in assorted lengths and colors are highly recommended so you don't have to make your own jumper wires. Newark #10R0135 (70 wires, $3.60), Newark #10R0134 (140 wires, $6.20), RadioShack #2760173 (140 wires, $6.99), or similar.

» 22-gauge solid wire, insulated, 15 feet minimum. Multiple colors are preferable but not necessary. Tayda Electronics sells black (#A-4994), white (#A-4995), red (#A-4996), yellow (#A-4997), green (#A-4998), and blue (#A-4999) for $0.10 per foot. (I suggest you get at least one foot each of red wire and either black or blue wire, and the rest in any color.)

This wire must be solid wire so you can plug it into your solderless breadboard. Do not purchase stranded wire because stranded wire is not meant to be plugged into a solderless breadboard. If you purchase a product called hookup wire, make sure that it is solid, not stranded, hookup wire.

» Alligator clips, fully insulated. Get one set of ten, preferably in assorted colors. RadioShack #2700378 (1 1/4-inch mini clips) or #2700356 (2-inch clips) or similar ($2.49–$3.49 per set). Also check online at Walmart, Amazon, or eBay.

» Two (minimum) 3-pin single-pole, double-throw slide switches (abbreviated as SPDT or 1P2T). Make sure these switches are breadboard friendly with pins spaced 0.1 inch (2.54 mm) apart. Tayda Electronics #A-5102 ($0.78 each).

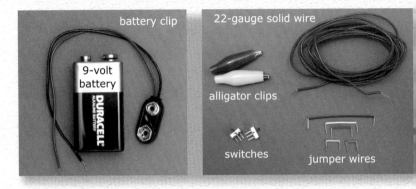

» **Resistors.** You'll need an assortment of resistor values (known as *resistances*). Look for carbon film resistors rated at 1/4 watt (W) or more with a tolerance of 20 percent or less.

Don't worry about the meaning of the type of resistor (that is, "carbon film"), the power rating (in watts), or the tolerance (a percentage). You just need this information for purchasing your resistors.

Listed next are the resistor values and the color codes used to identify them. You need only one or two resistors of each value, but suppliers sell resistors in packs of five, ten, or more, so purchase one pack of each. (Tayda Electronics sells ten-packs for $0.10 each. RadioShack sells five-packs for $1.49 each.) Here are the values you need:

» 330 ohm (orange-orange-brown)

» 470 ohm (yellow-violet-brown)

» 10 kohm (brown-black-orange)

» 47 kohm (yellow-violet-orange)

» 100 kohm (brown-black-yellow)

» 470 kohm (yellow-violet-yellow)

» 1 Mohm (brown-black-green)

» 4.7 Mohm (yellow-violet-green)

Ohms is the unit of measure for resistance. A kohm is 1,000 ohms and a Mohm is 1,000,000 ohms. Suppliers may list resistance values in Ω, kΩ, or MΩ, where Ω is the symbol for ohms.

» Capacitors

- » Two 0.01 μF Mylar film capacitors, rated for 16 volts (abbreviated V) or higher. Tayda Electronics #A-4106 ($0.04 each). (I recommend that you order four.)

- » One 4.7 μF electrolytic capacitor, rated for 16 V or higher. Tayda Electronics #A-4504 ($0.02 each). (I recommend that you order three.)

F is the abbreviation for farads, the unit of measure for capacitance. μF is the abbreviation for microfarads. A microfarad is 0.000001 farad.

» **LEDs.** Minimum quantities are specified in the following list, but I recommend you purchase at least a few more of each. (They're cheap — and they're fryable.)

- » Two 5 millimeter (mm) red LEDs. Tayda Electronics #A-1554 ($0.03 each). (I suggest you buy ten.)

- » One 5 mm green LED. Tayda Electronics #A-1553 ($0.03 each). (I suggest you buy five.)

- » One 5 mm ultrabright clear (white) LED. Tayda Electronics #A-408 ($0.05 each). (I suggest you buy five.)

» **Transistors.** Buy one or two extra of each type, just in case you fry one. They cost pennies each online, or $1.49 each in RadioShack stores.

- » One 2N3904 general-purpose NPN bipolar transistor. Tayda Electronics #A-111 ($0.02).

- » One 2N3906 general-purpose PNP bipolar transistor. Tayda Electronics #A-117 ($0.02).

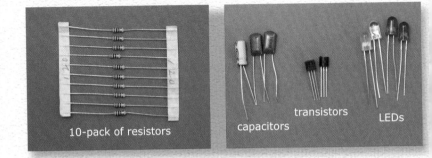

10-pack of resistors · capacitors · transistors · LEDs

» Miscellaneous

» One 555 timer integrated circuit (IC). This IC comes in a package known as an 8-pin DIP. Tayda Electronics #A-249 ($0.13 each). (Buy one or two extra.)

» One light-dependent resistor (LDR, or photoresistor), any value. Tayda Electronics #A-1528 ($0.24) or similar. (Buy one or two extra.)

» One 8-ohm, 0.5 W speaker. Tayda Electronics #A-4140 ($1.28), RadioShack #2730092 ($3.99), or similar.

» **Radio components.** Project 7, Radio, requires one inexpensive component and a couple of pricy components, one of which (the earphone) is not all that easy to find, because most electronics suppliers don't carry it.

» One 1N34/1N34A germanium diode. Tayda Electronics #A-1716 ($0.24). (Buy at least two.)

» One spool (at least 50 feet) of 24 gauge (AWG) magnet wire. Temco #MW0190 or similar. ($6.00–$15.00 online at Amazon or eBay.)

» One piezoelectric earphone (sometimes called a crystal earphone or a crystal radio earphone). This earphone may or may not come with a 3.5 mm plug at the end of the wires. (You don't need the plug, but if you buy one with a plug, you can just cut it off.) Amplified

Parts #P-A480 (with plug at AmplifiedParts.com, eBay, or Amazon), Mini Science #CH905ST (without plug at miniscience.com), or similar. Expect to pay about $10 including shipping.

TOOLS AND SUPPLIES

You need the following hand tools and other supplies to help you build your projects:

» **Solderless breadboard:** You use a solderless (pronounced "sodd-er-less") breadboard to build circuits. Purchase a breadboard that has 400 contact holes (also called tie points) and includes power rails (also called power lanes or bus lines), such as Tayda Electronics #A-1424 ($2.69) or RadioShack #2760003 ($9.99).

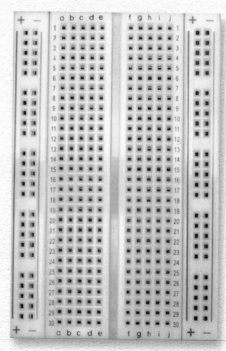

» **Wire stripper/cutter:** You use this tool to cut wires, trim component leads, and strip insulation from the end of wires. I recommend getting a gauged wire stripper/cutter, but you can use an adjustable wire stripper/cutter instead. Make sure your wire stripper can be adjusted to strip 22-gauge (22 AWG) wire. RadioShack #6400224 ($9.99) or similar. (Check your local hardware store or Walmart.)

» **Needle-nose pliers:** This handy tool helps you bend leads and wire and makes it easier to insert and remove components from your solderless breadboard. (Check your family's toolbox or get a set of 5-inch pliers for $6.00–$12.00 at a hardware store or Walmart.)

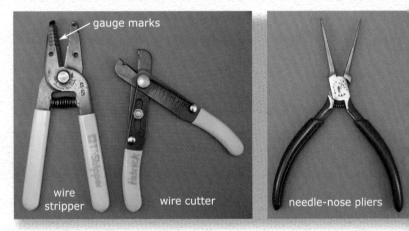

gauge marks

wire stripper wire cutter needle-nose pliers

» **Safety glasses:** Okay, so you risk looking a bit nerdy wearing safety glasses while you work on your electronics projects. But better to look nerdy than to not be able to look at all because the wire that you just clipped went flying into your eye. (Some of the 3M safety glasses are actually attractive and cost $3-$10 plus shipping on Amazon.com.)

» **Electrical tape:** You need about 4–6 inches of 3/4-inch electrical tape, such as Scotch #4218-BA-40. ($2-$6 per roll a Walmart, Home Depot, or other hardware stores.)

» **One 9-by-12-inch sheet of adhesive craft foam.** Check your local craft store (roughly $1.00). (Amazon and Walmart sell multipacks for $12.00–$15.00.)

» **One package of assorted grit sandpaper.** If you don't already have sandpaper, you can purchase it from any hardware store, Walmart, Amazon.com, and other suppliers ($5.00 or less).

» **Three paper fasteners.** You may have some fasteners at home, but if you don't, you can buy a box of 60-100 for about $3.00 at Walmart or any office supply store.

» **Spray or liquid glue:** You can purchase a container at Walmart or any craft store for $2-$5.

» **Assorted items.** Scissors, one toilet paper roll, one paper towel roll, aluminum foil, one sheet of plain white paper, transparent or masking tape, a ruler, one piece of cardboard or plastic lid, and a large coffee can or other large metal object.

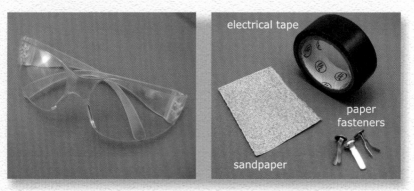

PROJECT 2 POCKET FLASHLIGHT

WOULD YOU LIKE TO CARRY A FLASHLIGHT IN YOUR POCKET?

You can pull it out, say, when you want to search for loose change under your sofa or to see the buttons on your TV remote while you're watching a movie in the dark.

Using just a few electronic parts and some craft materials, you can make a pocket flashlight with an on/off switch. Here are the parts and tools you need:

» One 9-volt battery

» One ultrabright clear 5 millimeter LED (which is short for *light-emitting diode*)

- One 470-ohm resistor (look for a stripe pattern of yellow, violet, brown, and then a fourth stripe of any color)

- A roll of 3/4-inch wide electrical tape (you need only about 4 inches in length from this roll)

- One 9-by-12-inch sheet of adhesive-backed craft foam (any color, plain or glitter foam)

- Scissors

- Needle-nose pliers

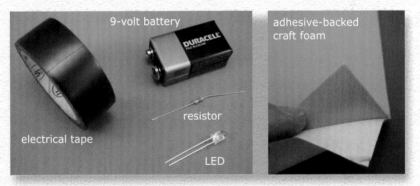

GET PREPARED

Before you start building your pocket flashlight, take a look at the three main electronic *components,* or parts, of your flashlight: the battery, the LED, and the resistor.

BATTERY

Can you guess why you need a battery for your pocket flashlight? Batteries store energy, and when you connect a battery to something that uses energy, the battery supplies the energy (until the battery runs out of energy). In your pocket flashlight, the battery provides the energy needed to light the LED.

Do you see the two metal pieces sticking out from the top of your 9-volt battery? Those metal pieces are the *terminals.* One terminal is positive and is labeled with a +. The other terminal is negative and isn't labeled. Note that the positive and negative terminals look different.

positive terminal

negative terminal

The battery voltage is a form of energy that exists between the two terminals. Voltage is measured in volts, which is abbreviated V.

Your battery's job is to supply 9 volts (or 9 V) to the other parts of your pocket flashlight, namely, the LED and the resistor.

LIGHT-EMITTING DIODE (LED)

Does your LED look like a typical light bulb? Well, it sure doesn't look like the kind of light bulb Thomas Edison worked with!

An LED gives off light when electric current passes through it. Electric current (or simply current) is the correct scientific term for what many people call electricity.

Note that two stiff wires are attached to the plastic case of your LED. Those wires are called *leads,* and they enable you to connect the LED to other electronic components.

When you connect your LED to a battery and a resistor in a complete path, or circuit, *current flows and the LED lights.*

Are the two leads of your LED the same length? They shouldn't be, and there's a good reason why they're not. The different lengths of the leads are a clue telling you which side of the LED is which. Here's why you need to know which side is which.

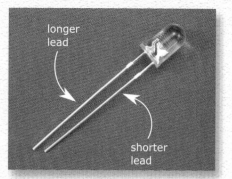

longer lead

shorter lead

LEDs are like one-way streets: They allow current to flow in one direction but not the other.

Because of this one-way current flow, you need to know which way to connect your LED in your flashlight circuit.

There's one more thing you need to know about LEDs: They can handle only a certain amount of current before they have a meltdown.

You should never connect a 9-volt battery directly to an LED. If you do, the battery's energy will push way too much current through the LED, and you may damage the LED.

RESISTOR

To protect your LED, you use a resistor to limit the current that flows through your flashlight circuit. *Resistors* slow down current, like a twist in a hose slows the flow of water. Every resistor has two leads.

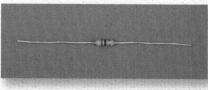

It doesn't matter which way you connect a resistor in a circuit because current flows either way through a resistor.

The colorful stripes on a resistor are a sort of code that tells you how much resistance the resistor provides. The higher the resistance, the more the resistor restricts current. Resistance is measured in ohms (which rhymes with homes).

For your pocket flashlight circuit, you need a 470-ohm resistor, which has a stripe pattern of yellow-violet-brown and then a fourth stripe of any color.

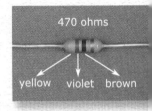

470 ohms

yellow   violet   brown

BUILD THE FLASHLIGHT CIRCUIT

To build your pocket flashlight circuit, you need to connect the battery, the resistor, and the LED in just the right way.

CONNECT THE RESISTOR TO THE BATTERY

Follow these steps to connect one side of the resistor to the positive terminal of the battery:

1 Bend one of the resistor leads around the positive battery terminal.

Use your needle-nose pliers to squeeze the resistor lead around the battery terminal.

2 Bend the resistor down from the positive battery terminal and wrap the resistor around the battery.

Use your needle-nose pliers to grip the positive battery terminal so you hold the attached resistor lead in place as you wrap the other end of the resistor around the battery.

3 Press the unconnected resistor lead down against the short edge of the battery, under the negative battery terminal.

WRAP TAPE AROUND THE POSITIVE TERMINAL

Electrical tape helps keep the resistor lead connected to the positive battery terminal, and keeps electronic components apart when you don't want them touching.

Use your scissors to cut a piece of electrical tape about 1 1/2 inches long. Then press the tape down onto and around the positive battery terminal, covering the resistor lead, too.

Make sure that both the positive battery terminal and the entire resistor lead are covered by the tape.

ADD A FOAM CUTOUT

Make and attach a foam cutout by following these steps:

1 **Cut out a 1-inch square piece of adhesive-backed foam.**

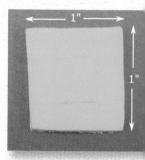

2 **Bend the foam in half and use scissors to cut two slits in the center of the square.**

3 **Carefully cut out the foam between the slits.**

There should be a hole in the foam that is about 1/2 inch high and about 1/4 inch wide.

 The size of the hole doesn't have to be exact.

4 **Remove the backing from the foam cutout.**

The sticky side of the foam is now exposed.

5 **Place the sticky side of the foam cutout on top of the unconnected resistor lead.**

Make sure the resistor lead is visible through the hole in the foam cutout.

6 **Press down the foam cutout to make it stick to the battery.**

CONNECT THE LED TO THE BATTERY

The last component to connect in your flashlight circuit is the LED. Follow these steps:

1 **Bend the shorter LED lead and wrap it around the negative battery terminal.**

Double-check which LED lead is the shorter lead. If you get it wrong, your flashlight circuit won't work.

Use your needle-nose pliers to squeeze the LED lead around the battery terminal.

2 **Bend the LED so that its plastic case is sticking up from the top of the battery near the edge.**

Hold the LED lead in place against the negative battery terminal as you bend the LED.

3 Position the LED.

While holding the LED's plastic case in place, bend the longer LED lead and position it so that it lies on top of the foam cutout.

The foam cutout should be between the resistor lead and the LED lead, preventing the two leads from touching. There should be a small gap between the two leads.

TIP

small gap between leads

WRAP TAPE AROUND THE NEGATIVE TERMINAL

Cut a piece of electrical tape about 1 1/2 inches long. Then press the tape down onto and around the negative battery terminal.

TEST YOUR CIRCUIT

Are you ready to test your flashlight circuit? If so, hold the battery in your hand and press down on the LED lead so that it touches the resistor lead that is under the foam cutout. (Don't worry. You won't get hurt!)

Does your LED light up? It should!

When the LED and resistor leads make contact, there is a connected path, or

circuit, and current flows out of the battery, through the resistor, through the LED, and back into the battery.

If your LED does not light up, don't worry. Take a deep breath and then check to see if the resistor and LED leads are making contact when you press down. If those leads are touching but your circuit is still not working, you may need to remove the electrical tape and check your other connections. Also, make sure that the shorter LED lead is connected to the negative battery terminal, and the longer LED lead is lined up over the foam cutout.

If your LED still doesn't light up, you may need to start over again using another battery and another LED.

ADD A COVER

Do you want to make a case for your pocket flashlight, so it looks like a real product? (This part of the project is optional.) To make a case, follow these steps:

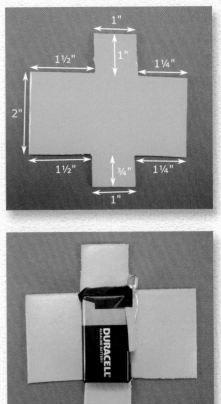

1 **Cut out a piece of adhesive-backed foam with dimensions chosen to fit your flashlight.**

2 **Remove the backing from the foam piece.**

3 **Lay the foam piece on a flat surface, with the sticky side up.**

4 **Place your pocket flashlight on the foam piece.**

Make sure the bottom edge of the battery is placed just above the lower rectangular section of the foam piece.

Press the battery into the foam.

5 **Wrap the lower rectangular section of the foam piece tightly around the bottom surface of the battery.**

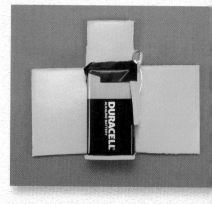

Press the section of foam firmly so it sticks to the bottom of the battery.

6 **Wrap the left and right sides of the foam piece around the sides and front of the battery.**

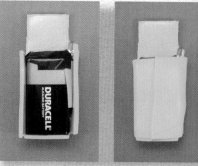

Press the foam sides firmly so they stick to the sides and front of the battery.

7 **Wrap the top of the foam piece around the top surface of the battery.**

Press the foam piece firmly so it sticks to the top of the battery.

8 **Locate and mark the spot you need to press to turn on the flashlight.**

The spot is on one of the sides of the battery, when the resistor and LED leads are lined up.

Use a Sharpie marker or pen to mark the spot.

This mark shows you where your flashlight's on/off switch is located.

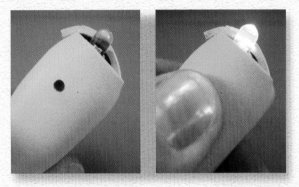

Why not make a few pocket flashlights for your friends or family members? Get creative and decorate your flashlight covers or use glitter craft foam for the cover. You may even be able to sell some!

PROJECT **3** RED LIGHT, GREEN LIGHT

HAVE YOU EVER SEEN A TWO-WAY TRAFFIC SIGNAL? It has a re
light (signaling stop) and a green light (signaling go). Two-way
traffic signals are used at toll booths, factory entrances, parking
lot exits, and other places where vehicles have to stop until a fee
is paid or there's room to move ahead.

Stop!

Pay the toll

Occupied

Go!

C'mon in!

Vacant

You can build a two-way traffic light circuit with just a few
electronic parts. Although you probably won't use your circuit
to control the flow of traffic, you might use it to signal to your
family when it's okay to come into your room — and when you
want to be left alone. A few other uses for a two-way traffic signa

are to let people know when a restroom is occupied or vacant, and to let pedestrians (that is, walkers) know whether they may cross a street or should stay put on the sidewalk.

BREADBOARDING

In this project, you use a solderless breadboard, or breadboard for short, to build your circuit. A *breadboard* is a rectangular plastic board that contains holes grouped in rows and columns. Rows are labeled with numbers and columns are labeled with letters or symbols.

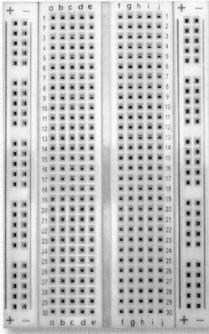

On certain breadboards, only some of the rows (such as 1, 5, 10, 15, 20, and so on) are labeled, but you should be able to figure out the number of each row.

Breadboards come in several sizes. You use a 400-hole breadboard for this project and others in this book.

The holes in a breadboard are called *contact holes*. Inside the board are strips of metal that connect groups of contact holes in patterns. By plugging in electronic components, such as resistors and LEDs, to certain contact holes, you can connect the electronic components. Attach a battery to the breadboard, and you can build a circuit quickly and easily.

Within each numbered row, the five holes in columns a, b, c, d, and e are connected, and the five holes in columns f, g, h, i, and j are connected. A sort of ditch runs down the center of the breadboard. The holes on the left side of the ditch are not connected to the holes on the right side of the ditch, and there are no connections between rows.

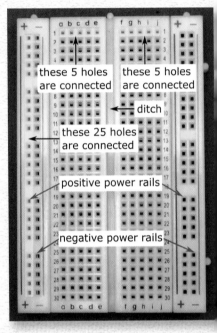

Running down the left and right sides of the breadboard are two pairs of columns labeled + and −. These outer columns are known as *power rails*. Within each power rail, every hole is connected to every other hole, but there are no connections between power rails.

You use the holes in the two center sections (columns a through j) to connect most of the components in your circuits. You use the power rails to connect your battery to other parts of your circuits.

GATHER SUPPLIES

For this project, you need the following electronic parts:

» Solderless breadboard

» One 9-volt battery

» One battery clip

» One 470-ohm resistor (yellow-violet-brown)

» One 5 mm red LED

» One 5 mm green LED

» Two single-pole, double-throw (SPDT) slide switches (for breadboard use)

» Two 1/4-inch (minimum) jumper wires (any color)

» Two 2-inch (minimum) jumper wires (any color, but preferably two different colors and ideally red and either black or blue)

You also need your wire cutter and needle-nose pliers.

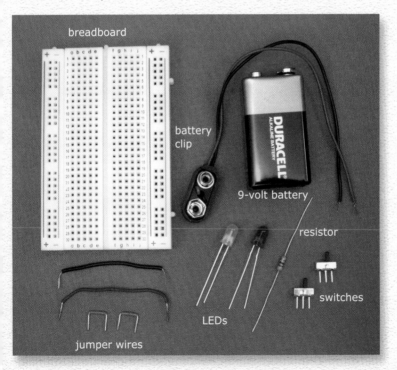

GET TO KNOW NEW PARTS

Before you start breadboarding your two-way traffic light circuit, take a look at these three electronic parts: a battery clip, a jumper wire, and an SPDT slide switch.

BATTERY CLIP

A *battery clip* (sometimes called a *snap connector*) contains two wires, or leads, that are electrically connected to the battery terminals when the clip is attached to the battery. The red lead is connected to the positive battery terminal and the black lead is connected to the negative battery terminal.

A battery clip makes it easier to connect your battery to your breadboard.

JUMPER WIRE

A *jumper wire* is a short insulated wire with ends that are bare (stripped of insulation).

You use jumper wires to connect two points in a breadboard circuit.

For this project, you need two 1/4-inch and two 2-inch jumper wires. In each case, the length refers to the minimum length of the main section of the jumper wire, not including the bare ends that you will stick into the breadboard holes.

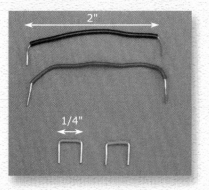

You can use longer jumper wires than the lengths specified, but shorter ones won't do.

For about $7, you can buy a box of precut jumper wires in assorted lengths and colors. Homemade wires are cheaper, but cutting and stripping them involves a bit of work.

If you'd like to make your own jumper wires, see the sidebar "How to Make a Jumper Wire" for step-by-step instructions and illustrations.

HOW TO MAKE A JUMPER WIRE

A *jumper wire* is a short insulated wire with bare (stripped of insulation) ends. You use jumper wires to connect two points in a breadboard circuit. Even if you have a set of precut jumper wires, you may need to make a jumper wire of a specific length for a circuit or two. Making a jumper wire isn't

(continued)

(continued)

that hard, as long as you have the right wire, tools, and a little patience.

You start with a reel (or long piece) of 22-gauge insulated wire. The *gauge* (pronounced "gage") of a wire is a measure of its diameter. In North America, the gauge is often labeled AWG (for American wire gauge). 22-gauge wire is thick enough — but not too thick — to fit into the contact holes of your breadboard.

You also need a wire cutter and a wire stripper, or one tool that does both jobs, as well as needle-nose pliers. You'll find it much easier to make jumper wires if your wire stripper has a gauge-selection dial or several cutting notches labeled for various gauges.

Gauged devices allow you to strip insulation without worrying about cutting the wire underneath the insulation.

If you use a generic wire stripper, you have to be very careful not to *nick* (accidentally cut into) the wire when you're stripping it. Nicks weaken the wire, and a weak wire can get stuck inside a breadboard hole and ruin your whole day.

To make your own jumper wire, follow these steps:

1 **Cut the wire to the length you need, using a wire-cutting tool.**

   If you need, say, a 2-inch jumper wire, cut a length of wire that is at least 2 3/4-inches long, so you leave room to strip some insulation off each end. It's better to cut a longer length of wire and trim it down if you need to than to cut a shorter length of wire and find that it's too short for your circuit.

2 Strip about 1/4 inch to 1/3 inch of insulation from each end.

If you use a gauged wire stripper, follow these steps:

a. Dial the gauge to 22 or locate the notch that is labeled 22.

b. With the jaws of the wire stripper open, place the wire in the appropriate notch of the wire stripper, so that roughly 1/4 to 1/3 inch of the wire extends past the wire stripper.

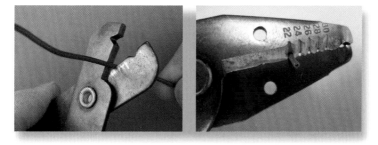

c. Firmly grip the wire stripper — as if you're trying to cut through the wire — while twisting and pulling the wire through the stripping tool. The insulation should come off but the wire should remain intact.

(continued)

(continued)

If you use a generic
wire stripper, follow
these steps:

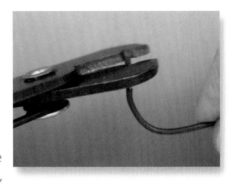

   a. Place the
   end of the
   wire into
   the cutting
   blades of the
   wire stripper,
   so that roughly 1/4 to 1/3 inch of the wire
   extends past the wire stripper.

   b. Grip the wire stripper just enough to begin
   cutting through the insulation. (If you grip it too
   tightly, you will nick or cut through the wire. If
   you don't grip it tightly enough, you won't cut
   through the insulation at all.)

   c. Release your grip on the wire stripper, rotate
   the wire a quarter turn, and then grip the wire
   stripper again with just enough pressure to
   begin cutting through the insulation.

   d. Rotate and repeat Steps b and c two or three
   more times, until you have nicked the insulation
   all the way around the wire.

   e. Grip the wire stripper — but not too tightly —
   around the nicked insulation while pulling
   on the other end of the wire to force the
   insulation off.

3 **Bend the exposed ends of wire at a right (90°) angle.**

Use your needle-nose pliers to do this.

With a little practice, you'll become an expert in making jumper wires!

SLIDE SWITCH

A single-pole, double-throw (SPDT) slide switch has three prongs, or *terminals,* and a *slider,* which is the black knob that moves back and forth between two positions.

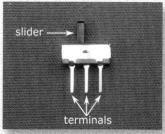

slider →

terminals

REMEMBER

The position of the slider determines which pair of terminals is connected inside the switch. For each position, a connection is made between the two terminals closest to the slider.

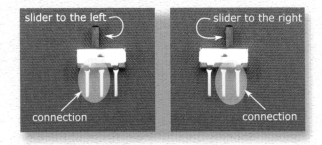

slider to the left

connection

slider to the right

connection

In this project, you use one SPDT slider switch to connect either the red LED or the green LED to your circuit. You use the other SPDT slider switch (in this and other projects) to either connect or disconnect the battery from your circuit.

BREADBOARD YOUR CIRCUIT

Follow these steps to build the two-way traffic light circuit on your breadboard:

1 **Bend and trim the 470-ohm resistor (yellow-violet-brown) leads.**

Wear safety glasses to avoid harm from fast-flying clipped leads.

Use your needle-nose pliers to bend the resistor leads down away from the body of the resistor. Then use the sharp scissorlike part of your wire cutters to clip each resistor lead so that about 1/4 inch of the lead is sticking down below the bend.

Each lead should be just long enough to reach from the top surface of the breadboard to the bottom.

2 **Insert the 470-ohm resistor into the breadboard.**

Plug one resistor lead into hole **11a** (that is, the hole in row 11, column a). Plug the other resistor lead into the positive power rail to the left of row **11.**

It doesn't matter which way you orient the resistor in your circuit, so you may plug either lead into hole 11a and the other lead into the positive power rail.

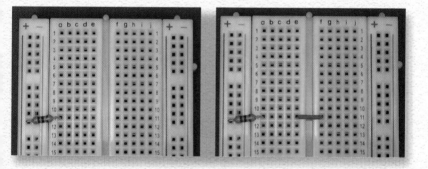

3 **Insert one of the 1/4-inch (or longer) jumper wires into the breadboard.**

Plug one end of the jumper wire into hole **11e** and the other end into hole **11f.**

This jumper wire connects the two sides of row 11, so now all ten contact holes in row 11 (holes 11a-11j) are electrically connected.

4 Bend and trim the leads of each LED.

Use your needle-nose pliers to bend the LED leads out and down, bending the positive (longer) lead out a bit more than the negative (shorter) lead. Then use your wire cutter to clip the LED leads so that the length of each lead is about 1/4 inch below the bend.

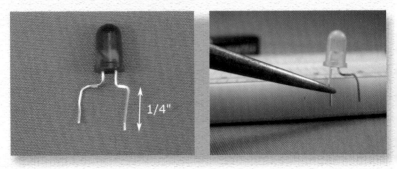

5 Insert the trimmed red LED into the breadboard.

You must orient the LED properly. Otherwise, it won't work.

Plug the positive side of the red LED into hole **10j.** Plug the negative side into the hole in the negative power rail to the right of row **10** on your breadboard.

If you don't know which lead was longer before you clipped the leads, take a peek inside the LED case to see the two pieces of metal attached to the leads. The larger piece of metal is on the negative side (also known as the cathode) and the smaller piece of metal is on the positive side (also known as the anode). Also, the edge of the red plastic case is flat on the negative side.

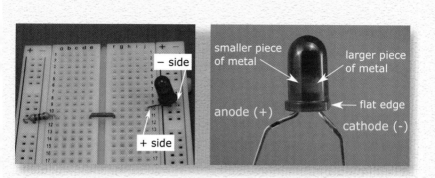

6 Insert the trimmed green LED into the breadboard.

Plug the positive side (smaller piece of metal) into hole *12j.*
Plug the negative side (larger piece of metal, flat edge) into
the hole in the negative power rail to the right of row *12* on
your breadboard.

7 Insert one of the switches into the breadboard.

Plug the three terminals of the SPDT switch into holes *10h,*
11h, and *12h.*

*It doesn't matter which way you orient the switch.
Upside down and right side up are both okay.*

This switch connects either the red LED or the green LED
to the 470-ohm resistor in row 11, through the jumper wire
inserted in Step 3. Let's call this the *LED selector switch* for
this circuit. Move the slider to the upper position (toward
row 1 of your breadboard).

8 **Connect the 9-volt battery to the breadboard.**

   a. Snap the battery clip onto the battery terminals.

   b. Carefully insert the black battery lead (negative terminal) into the top hole in the negative power rail on the right.

   You are connecting the negative battery terminal to the negative side of both LEDs, because all the holes in the negative power rail are connected.

   c. Carefully insert the red battery lead (positive terminal) into the top hole in the positive power rail on the left.

   You are connecting the positive battery terminal to one side of the 470-ohm resistor because all the holes in the positive power rail are connected.

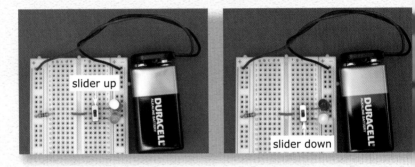

Does the red LED light? If it does, congratulations! You've successfully breadboarded your first circuit! Now, move the slider on the LED selector switch. Does the green LED light? If so, you now have a working two-way traffic light!

TRACK DOWN PROBLEMS

If one or both of your LEDs did not light, go back and review the steps for building your circuit. Here are some questions to ask yourself as you *troubleshoot,* or track down, the source of the problem with your circuit:

» Is each component inserted into the correct hole in your breadboard?

» Are all the leads pushed firmly, but not excessively, into your breadboard?

» Is the battery clip snapped firmly onto the battery terminals?

» Are your LEDs oriented correctly?

» Did one (or both) of your LEDs go kaput somehow? (If you're not sure, try using new LEDs.)

WHAT'S REALLY HAPPENING?

When you plug electronic components into your breadboard, your breadboard makes connections between components. By moving the slider on the switch back and forth, your switch connects either the red or the green LED to your circuit. Electric current flows along the path of the connections, and the LED selected by the switch lights.

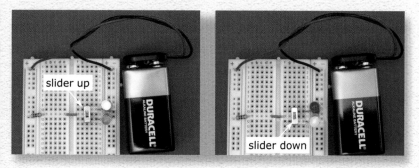

IMPROVE YOUR CIRCUIT

Your two-way traffic light circuit works fine the way it is, but there are a couple of things you can do to make it easier to use. And once you make these changes, you'll find it easier to build the other projects in this book.

CONNECT THE POWER RAILS

You use the power rails to connect parts of your circuit to your battery. It's much easier to breadboard circuits when you can make connections to power on either the right or the left side of the breadboard.

Grab the 2-inch jumper wires you set aside at the beginning of this project. Leave your two-way traffic light circuit set up. Then follow these steps to connect the power rails:

1 **Connect one jumper wire (preferably black or blue) between the two negative power rails in the last row of your breadboard.**

2 **Connect the other jumper wire (preferably red) between the two positive power rails in the second-to-last row of your breadboard.**

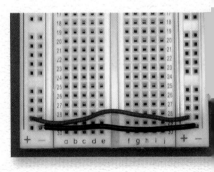

Now all the contact holes in the left negative power rail are connected to all the contact holes in the right negative power rail, and all the contact holes in the left positive power rail are connected to all the contact holes in the right positive power rail.

It's time to test your power rail connections. Follow these steps:

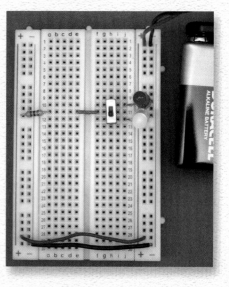

1 Remove the red battery lead from the top hole in the positive rail on the left.

Both LEDs should be off now because the battery has been removed from the circuit.

2 Place the red battery lead in the top hole in the positive power rail on the right.

The LED selected by your LED selector switch should light.

It's a good idea to leave these power rail connections in place whenever you breadboard a circuit. That way, you always have access to both battery terminals on both sides of your breadboard.

ADD A POWER SWITCH

To preserve battery power, you can add a power switch to your circuit. Grab the remaining parts for this project, an SPDT slide switch and a 1/4-inch jumper wire. Leave your two-way traffic circuit set up, and follow these steps to add the power switch:

1 Move the red battery lead.

Remove the red battery lead from the positive power rail on the right and connect it to hole **2j.**

2 **Insert the 1/4-inch jumper wire.**

Plug one end of the jumper wire into hole **3j**. Plug the other end of the jumper wire into the hole in the positive power rail to the right of row **3**.

3 **Insert the switch.**

Plug the three terminals of the switch into holes **2h**, **3h**, and **4h**. (It doesn't matter which way you orient the switch.)

Test your power switch by moving the slider on the switch back and forth. Does one of the LEDs in your circuit turn on and off?

Here's how the circuit works with the switch in place:

» With the slider in the lower position, the battery is disconnected from the circuit, so the LEDs are off.

» With the slider in the upper position, the battery is connected to the circuit, so one of the LEDs is on. (Which LED is on depends on the position of the LED selector switch.)

With every circuit you build, it's a good idea to use a power switch to connect and disconnect your battery. So leave the switch and jumper wire in place for the other breadboard projects in this book.

DO YOU USE A NIGHTLIGHT TO BRIGHTEN A BATHROOM, YOUR BEDROOM, OR A DARK HALLWAY? Nightlights are often credited with preventing sleepyheads from tripping over or walking into things in the dark. The only thing better than a nightlight is a smart nightlight that knows when to turn itself on and when to save electricity by turning itself off.

In this project, you discover how easy it is to build a nightlight with brains. Well, actually, your brainy nightlight doesn't have brains, or even a microprocessor, which is the electronic equivalent of a brain. But your nightlight does have something called a *sensor*, which detects the amount of light shining on it and, um, uses its senses to figure out when to turn on and when to turn off. So you might say that this nightlight has a certain amount of common sense.

COLLECT PARTS

For this project, you need the following electronic parts:

» Solderless breadboard, prepared with a

   » 9-volt battery with battery clip

   » Power switch and jumper wire

   » Power rail jumper-wire connections

» One photoresistor (also called light-dependent resistor, or LDR)

» One 2N3904 NPN bipolar transistor

» One 2N3906 PNP bipolar transistor

» One 330-ohm resistor (orange-orange-brown)

» One 10-kohm (which is 10,000 ohms) resistor (brown-black-orange)

» One 1-Mohm (which is 1,000,000 ohms) resistor (brown-black-green)

» One 5 mm clear, white LED

» Two 5/16-inch (minimum) jumper wires (any color)

» Additional resistors may be required to make adjustments to the circuit:

   » One 100-kohm (100,000 ohms) resistor (brown-black-yellow)

   » One 470-kohm (470,000 ohms) resistor (yellow-violet-yellow)

   » One 4.7-Mohm (4,700,000 ohms) resistor (yellow-violet-green)

The prefix kilo *(abbreviated k) means thousands, so a kilohm (or kohm) is 1,000 ohms. The prefix* mega *(abbreviated M) means millions, so a megohm (or Mohm) is 1,000,000 ohms.*

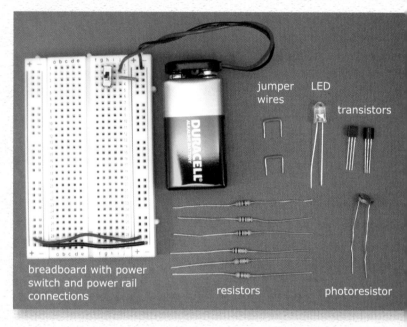

jumper wires

LED

transistors

breadboard with power switch and power rail connections

resistors

photoresistor

You also need your wire cutter to trim leads, and you may want to use your needle-nose pliers to insert and remove components.

A SIMPLE SENSOR

Have you ever noticed an outdoor light (like, say, on a front porch or over a garage) turning on when you walk near it? If so, chances are you've experienced a *motion detector* or *motion sensor*. Sensors acts like our five senses: They detect physical sensations, such as light, heat, motion, or sound, and respond in some way.

A *photoresistor* is one kind of light sensor. It acts like a resistor except that the value of resistance depends on how much light is shining on it. Photoresistors are also known as *light-dependent resistors (LDRs)* or *photocells*.

It's hard to know the exact resistance of a photoresistor unless you know exactly how much light is shining on it. But that's okay. You don't need to know the exact resistance. You just need to know *about* how much resistance a photoresistor has in darkness and in bright light.

In general, a photoresistor works like this:

» In bright light, its resistance is relatively low (usually less than 10 kohms).

» In darkness, its resistance is relatively high (usually more than 1 Mohm).

To remember how a photoresistor works, think of opposites. When the light level is high, the resistance is low. When the light level is low, the resistance is high.

Your nightlight circuit is designed to use this change in resistance to either allow or restrict the flow of current through an LED so that the LED either lights or doesn't light, depending on how dark or bright the room is.

THE TINY, YET POWERFUL, TRANSISTOR

A *transistor* is a tiny electronic device that has three leads and can do some amazing things. The two main jobs of a transistor are the following:

» It acts like a tiny automatic switch. A transistor can do the same job as the SPDT slide switch you use in Project 3 — except you don't have to move a slider to get it to switch. The transistor automatically does the switching for you.

» It boosts, or *amplifies,* electric current. When you send a tiny current into one of the transistor's leads, a larger current flows through the other two transistor leads.

Transistors look really dull and boring, but because of the important jobs they do, they are used in nearly every electronic device in the world. For instance, the Apple iPhone 6 contains over 2 billion transistors! (Of course, the transistors used in phones, TVs, computers, and most other electronic devices are microscopic in size and don't look anything like the ones you use in this project. But they work the same way!)

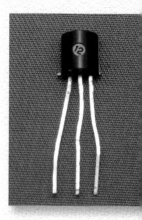

TRANSISTORS AND FAUCETS

Have you ever thought about what happens when you turn on a faucet? (What! No? You mean you don't spend time thinking about faucets? Shocking!) Here's what happens:

» By turning the handle, you switch the water on or off.

» By adjusting how much you turn the handle, you control how much water flows.

Do those two functions of a faucet sound a little like the two jobs of a transistor?

A transistor acts, in a way, like a faucet for electric current. One part of the transistor — the *base* — controls the flow of current between the other two parts of the transistor — the *collector* and the *emitter.*

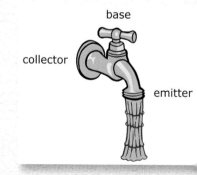

base

collector

emitter

When you apply enough pressure, or energy, to a faucet handle, you switch the faucet on and water flows. Likewise, when you apply enough voltage, or energy, to the base of a transistor, you switch the transistor on and current flows from the collector to the emitter.

If you don't apply enough pressure, or energy, to the faucet handle, the faucet is off and no water flows. Similarly, if the voltage at the base of a transistor is too low, the transistor is off and no current flows.

When the faucet is on, you control the amount of water flowing through it by adjusting the handle. When a transistor is switched on, you control the amount of current that flows from the collector to the emitter by controlling how much current flows into the base of the transistor.

Don't worry about the details of exactly how to control a transistor. The nightlight circuit will take care of the details for you.

EXPLORE TWO TRANSISTORS

Just as different models of iPhones perform the same functions (for instance, call, text, browse the Internet, and take pictures) but differ in terms of speed and other features, different models of transistors perform the same functions (switch and amplify) but differ in terms of speed and other features.

In your nightlight circuit, you use two models of transistors: an NPN 2N3904 transistor and a PNP 2N3906 transistor. (Catchy names, eh? Too bad they're not called iTransistor 1 and iTransistor 2!) The model number is stamped on the

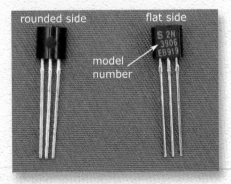

rounded side   flat side

model number

flat side of the transistor case (that black plastic blob on top of the leads is the case).

Both the 2N3904 and the 2N3906 transistors have three leads, or terminals, which are often called *pins*. Each pin connects to the base, collector, or emitter inside the transistor case. Like LEDs, transistors are picky about which way they are placed in a circuit. So you have to know which lead, or pin, is which.

You identify the pins by looking at a *pin diagram,* or *pinout.* Transistors sold by RadioShack provide the pinout on the outside of the transistor's cardboard packaging.

Pin diagram viewed from bottom

Collector ———

Base ———

Emitter ———

TO-92 case

Don't be confused if you see a reference to TO-92 in a pinout. That label identifies the packaging, *or type of case, in which the transistor is housed. TO-92 is not a model number.*

The pinout is always shown on the transistor's datasheet, which you can find on the Internet. The *datasheet* is a rather unfriendly technical document that lists all the features and specifications of the transistor. (Don't let the datasheet intimidate you! Just look for the pin diagram. That's all you need to worry about.)

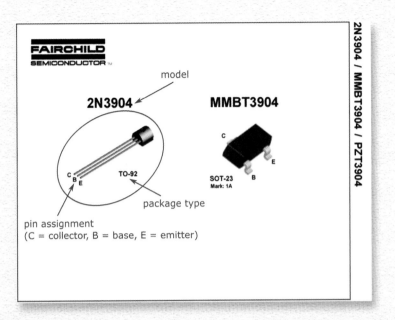

2N3904 / MMBT3904 / PZT3904

model

2N3904

MMBT3904

C

E

C
B
E

TO-92

SOT-23
Mark: 1A

B

package type

pin assignment
(C = collector, B = base, E = emitter)

Websites that sell electronic parts often include a link to the datasheet from the product page for the transistor.

If you can't locate the datasheet, you can search the Internet for a particular transistor model's pinout. For instance, search for 2N3904 pinout.

Depending on where you get your transistors, the pinout may not be the same as the standard pinout used by most manufacturers. Be sure to check the packaging or documentation that comes with your transistor to determine which pin is which.

standard pinout for 2N3904, 2N3906 · collector · base · emitter

flat side

When you plug your transistor into your solderless breadboard as you build the nightlight circuit, make sure that you orient the transistor correctly. It matters — very much — how you connect the base, collector, and emitter of a transistor.

Ready to build your brainy nightlight circuit?

BUILD THE CIRCUIT

In this project, you use your photoresistor to sense how much light there is in the room and to control whether the two transistors are switched on or off. When the transistors are switched on, they allow current to flow through an LED. The transistors also amplify the current so that it is strong enough to light the LED brightly.

Follow these steps to build your nightlight circuit:

1 **Double-check your solderless breadboard.**

    a. Make sure that the two positive power rails are connected and the two negative power rails are connected.

b. Check that your power switch and jumper wire connections are properly installed and that the switch is in the off position.

c. Verify that the leads from your battery clip are snugly plugged into the correct contact holes in your breadboard.

2 **Insert the 1-Mohm resistor (brown-black-green) into the breadboard.**

Bend and trim the resistor leads so that each lead is about 3/8 inch long below the bend. Then plug one lead into hole **13a** and the other lead into a hole in the positive power rail to the left of row **13**.

3 **Insert a 5/16-inch (minimum) jumper wire into the breadboard.**

Plug one end of the jumper wire into hole **15a** and the other end of the jumper wire into a hole in the negative power rail to the left of row **15**.

4 Insert the 2N3904 NPN transistor into the breadboard.

a. Double-check that you have selected a 2N3904 transistor. (If you mix up the transistors, your circuit won't work.)

b. Use your needle-nose pliers to gently bend the transistor pins out and down.

c. Hold the transistor so that its pins are facing down and the flat part of the transistor case is facing right.

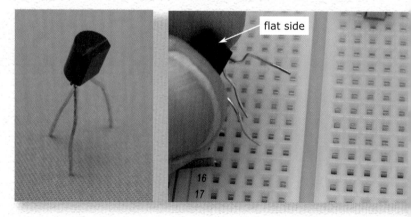

flat side

d. Using your fingers or needle-nose pliers to gently move the pins, position the collector (top) pin into the opening to hole **11d**, the base (middle) pin into the opening to hole **13c**, and the emitter (bottom) pin into the opening to hole **15d**.

If your 2N3904 transistor uses a different pin assignment than mine, you may need to orient the transistor differently to get the right pins positioned over the correct holes.

e. Holding the transistor by its case, gently push down on the transistor, rocking it back and forth as you push down, until each pin is plugged in firmly, but not excessively.

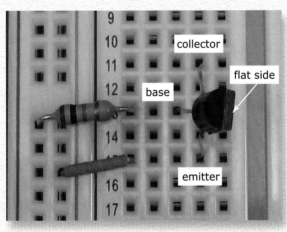

5 Insert the photoresistor into the breadboard.

Plug one lead (either one) into hole **13b** and the other lead into any hole in the negative power rail on the left side of the board. (I used the hole to the left of row **17.**)

6 Insert the 10-kohm resistor (brown-black-orange) into the breadboard.

Bend and trim the resistor leads. Then plug one lead into hole **11e** and the other lead into hole **11f.**

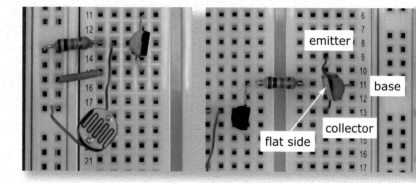

7 **Insert the 2N3906 PNP transistor into the breadboard.**

a. Double-check that you have selected a 2N3906 transisto[r]

b. Use your needle-nose pliers to gently bend the transisto[r] pins out and down.

c. Hold the transistor so that its pins are facing down and the flat part of the transistor case is facing left.

d. Plug the emitter (top) pin into the opening to hole **9h,** the base (middle) pin into the opening to hole **11j,** and the collector (bottom) pin into the opening to hole **13h.**

If your 2N3906 transistor uses a different pin assignment than mine, you may need to orient the transistor differently to get the right pins positioned over the right holes.

8 Insert a 5/16-inch (minimum) jumper wire into the breadboard.

Plug one end of the jumper wire into hole **9j** and the other end of the jumper wire into the positive power rail to the right of row **9.**

9 Insert the LED into the breadboard.

a. Trim the LED leads so that they are at least 1/2-inch long from end to end.

b. Plug the cathode (negative side, flat edge, larger piece of metal inside the case) into hole **15f** and the anode (positive side) into hole **13f.**

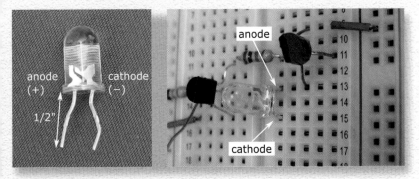

10 **Insert the 330-ohm resistor (orange-orange-brown) into the breadboard.**

   a. Bend and trim the resistor leads.

   b. Plug one lead into hole **15j** and the other lead into the negative power rail to the right of row **15.**

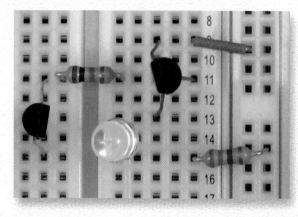

Double-check all your connections and the orientation of your LED. Make sure you have the 2N3904 NPN transistor on the left side of your breadboard and the 2N3906 PNP transistor on the right side of your breadboard. When you are sure that your circuit is set up correctly, it's time to try it out!

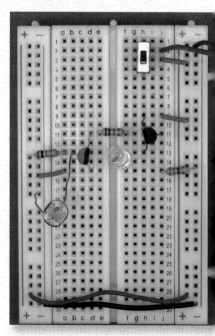

TEST YOUR NIGHTLIGHT CIRCUIT

The best place to test out your circuit is in a room that has shades, blinds, or other window coverings. (But don't worry if you have no way to darken the room. You can still test your circuit.)

With the room lights on (or sunlight shining into the room), turn on the power switch. Did the LED light up? It shouldn't. If it does, you can make adjustments to the circuit, as described in the next section.

If the LED did not light up, that's good!

Now, turn off the lights (or block the sunlight from coming in the windows). Did the LED light up? It should!

If your brainy nightlight circuit works as it should, give yourself a pat on the back for successfully building your first circuit that uses a sensor.

But don't worry if the LED does not light up when the lights are off. Chances are you just need to make a small change to your circuit, as described in the next section.

To determine what change is required, you need to run a little test. With the power switch on and the room darkened, use your fingers to cover the top or the top and sides of the photoresistor so that little or no light gets in. Note whether or not your LED turns on. Then move on to the next section.

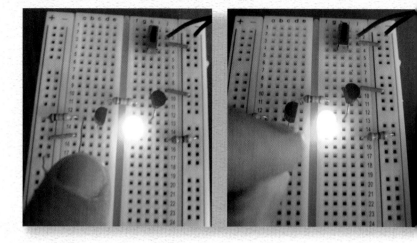

MAKE ADJUSTMENTS

If your nightlight circuit doesn't work (the LED doesn't turn on when it's relatively dark in the room, or the LED turns on when the light in the room is bright or fairly bright), you can adjust your circuit. Making changes is common in a circuit like this because the level of light in a room can vary quite a bit and each photoresistor is a little different in terms of sensitivity to light.

Before you make any changes to your circuit, turn off the power switch.

REMEMBER

Make an adjustment based on which of the following problem conditions you are experiencing.

NIGHTLIGHT TURNS ON WHEN IT SHOULDN'T

If your nightlight turns on when it shouldn't (that is, when there's quite a bit of light in the room), you may be able to solve the problem by using a larger value of resistance in place of the 1-Mohm resistor.

Remove the 1-Mohm resistor (row 13 on the left side of the board) and replace it with the 4.7-Mohm resistor (yellow-violet-green) on the parts list. (Remember to trim and bend the leads of the 4.7-Mohm resistor before inserting it into the breadboard.)

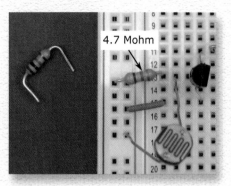

4.7 Mohm

Increasing the resistance increases the light sensitivity of the circuit so that your room must be darker to turn on the LED.

After you swap resistors, turn on the power switch and test the circuit again.

NIGHTLIGHT DOESN'T TURN ON WHEN IT SHOULD

If your nightlight doesn't turn on when the room is fairly dark, but it does turn on when you cover the photoresistor with your fingers, try the following. Remove the 1-Mohm resistor (row 13) and replace it with the 470-kohm resistor (yellow-violet-yellow), after trimming and bending the resistor leads.

Decreasing the resistance decreases the light sensitivity of the circuit so that your room doesn't have to be quite so dark to turn on the LED.

After swapping resistors, turn on the power switch and test the circuit again.

If your nightlight still doesn't turn on when the room is fairly dark, you can try one more thing. Turn off the power switch, replace the 470-kohm resistor (row 13) with the 100-kohm resistor (brown-black-yellow) from your parts list, turn on the power switch, and test the circuit again.

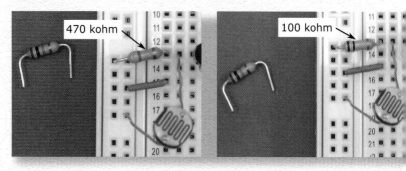

470 kohm

100 kohm

NIGHTLIGHT DOESN'T TURN ON AT ALL

If your nightlight doesn't turn on at all — even when you cover the photoresistor — it's time to troubleshoot your circuit to figure out what's wrong. Here's what to look for:

» Is your power switch on? (Don't laugh; I neglected to turn on the power switch while testing my circuit for this project, and scratched my head for a few minutes before I figured out what was wrong!)

» Is your LED oriented correctly (as specified in Step 9 earlier in this project)?

» Is the transistor on the left side of the board a 2N3904 NPN transistor? Is the flat side of this transistor case facing right (assuming your transistor uses a standard pin assignment)? Are the collector, base, and emitter leads firmly plugged into the correct breadboard holes (as specified in Step 4)?

» Is the transistor on the right side of the board a 2N3906 PNP transistor? Is the flat side of this transistor case facing left (assuming your transistor uses a standard pin assignment)? Are the collector, base, and emitter leads firmly plugged into the correct breadboard holes (as specified in Step 7)?

» Are all components and jumper wires inserted firmly, but not excessively, into the correct breadboard holes?

If, after trying everything in the preceding checklist, your circuit is still not working, use a fresh 9-volt battery.

Still not working? Replace the photoresistor in your circuit, if you have another one.

If you replace the photoresistor, you may have to try different values of resistance in place of the resistor in row 13 to adjust the light sensitivity of the circuit.

If your nightlight is still not working properly, replace one or both transistors. Transistors are sensitive electronic devices that are easily damaged — but they don't give off smoke or provide other evidence of failure. It's really hard to tell whether or not a transistor is okay.

If you discover that you have a bad transistor, throw it in the trash right away so you don't mistakenly use it in another circuit.

HAVE YOU EVER SEEN A RAILROAD CROSSING SIGN WITH ALTERNATING FLASHING RED LIGHTS? With just a handful of electronic components, you can build a circuit that simulates (that is, imitates) the action of a flashing railroad crossing sign.

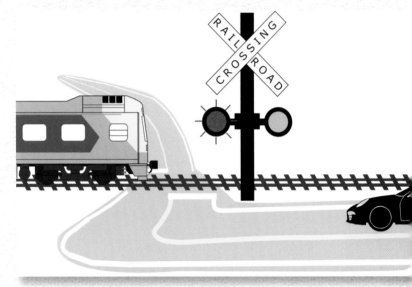

Among the components you use to build your circuit are two new (to you) types of electronic components: a capacitor (actually, two capacitors) and an integrated circuit. So let's start by taking a look at these new components.

WHAT'S A CAPACITOR?

A *capacitor* (pronounced "cuh-PAA-sih-ter") is a pretty simple electronic device. It consists of two electrical conductors (known as *plates*) that are separated by a special type of insulator (that is a nonconductor) known as a *dielectric* (pronounced "die-ih-LECK-trick"). Leads are attached to each plate and a coating or other case is placed around the capacitor.

Capacitors come in a variety of shapes, size, and colors. On some capacitors, the leads stick out from the bottom of the case and are known as *radial* leads. On other capacitors, the leads stick out from the ends of the case and are known as *axial* leads. The way the leads are attached doesn't affect the functioning of the capacitor.

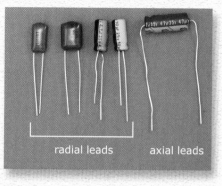

radial leads   axial leads

Capacitor plates and the dielectric can be made from a variety of materials, so different kinds of capacitors have different qualities and uses. Capacitors, or *caps* as they are often called, are used in many ways in a circuit.

Two of the most important jobs a capacitor can do are

» **Store electrical energy:** A capacitor can act like a temporary battery, providing energy to other components in a circuit even when there is no battery or other voltage source.

» **Create a timer:** Working with one or more resistors, a capacitor can control the amount of time it takes for an event, such as the sounding of a buzzer or the lighting of an LED, to occur in a circuit.

In your railroad crossing sign, the main job of the capacitors is to help create the timer that controls the flashing of two red LEDs.

The value of a capacitor is known as its capacitance. *Capacitance* is a measure of how much energy a capacitor can store.

Capacitance is measured in units called farads *(abbreviated F), but the capacitors you use in this project have capacitances in the microfarad (abbreviated μF) range. One* microfarad *equals one millionth of a farad.*

CHECK OUT YOUR CAPACITORS

You use a 0.01 microfarad (μF) film capacitor and a 4.7 μF electrolytic capacitor in this project. Film capacitors are *nonpolarized*, which means it doesn't matter which way you connect their leads in a circuit. Electrolytic capacitors are *polarized*,

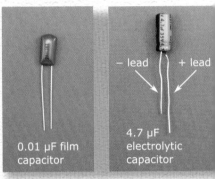

− lead   + lead

0.01 μF film capacitor

4.7 μF electrolytic capacitor

which means the way you connect their leads in a circuit matters.

To tell which side of an electrolytic capacitor is which, look for a large stripe or a minus sign (or both) on one side of the cap. The lead closest to that stripe or minus sign is the negative lead, and the other lead (which is unlabeled) is the positive lead. The shorter lead is the negative lead and the longer lead is the positive lead.

If you clip the leads of an electrolytic capacitor, you can still look for the stripe or minus sign to identify the negative lead.

The value of most electrolytic capacitors is marked on the case. Other types of capacitors, including the 0.01 μF film capacitor you use in the project, are so small that there's not enough room for the value, so the case is marked with a code that identifies the value. The code for your 0.01 μF film capacitor is 103 and may be followed by a letter.

A marking of 4.7μF 35V on an electrolytic capacitor tells you that the capacitance is 4.7 μF and the maximum voltage that this capacitor should be exposed to is 35 V. This project uses a 9 V battery, so a 35 V voltage rating is fine (and a capacitor rated for 16 V works too).

 If you use a capacitor rated for a lower voltage than the power supply in your circuit, you risk damaging your capacitor.

WHAT'S AN INTEGRATED CIRCUIT?

Individual electronic components, such as resistors, capacitors, LEDs, and transistors, are known as *discrete components*. You connect discrete components as you build your circuit. An *integrated circuit (IC)* contains anywhere from a few dozen to many billions (yes — billions!) of circuit components packed in a single device that can fit into the palm of your hand.

The components in an IC are connected to form a miniature circuit that performs one or more functions, such as counting or adding two numbers. Among the most complex ICs are the *microprocessors* that do most of the work involved in running your smartphone, tablet, laptop, and other products. Microprocessors perform many functions and are often called the brains of computing.

ICs, which are often called *chips,* come in a plastic case (which is usually black) with pins sticking out. Hidden from view inside the plastic case is the tiny circuit. The *pins* are used to connect parts of the tiny circuit to the world

outside the IC. ICs commonly used in basic electronics typically have 8, 14, or 16 pins, while advanced microprocessors have hundreds of pins! The IC you use in this project has just 8 pins.

Because an IC doesn't have a power source, at least two pins on every IC are used to connect a battery or other power source to the circuit inside the chip. The chip is typically part of an every larger circuit: By connecting the leads of discrete components to the chip's pins, you create one big happy circuit!

Every chip has a model number (among other things) stamped on its case. The model number identifies the chip's function. Thousands of different ICs are available today, and each one has a datasheet that tells you exactly what it does, how much power it needs, and what each of its pins is used for. You won't need the datasheet for the IC in this project because I tell you exactly how to use the chip in your railroad crossing circuit.

PAY ATTENTION TO THE PINOUT!

Never — never! — make random connections to IC pins thinking you can simply explore different ways to get the chip to work.

Because every IC model is different, each pin diagram, or *pinout*, is different, too. The pinout tells you the pin assignment, or how each pin is used inside the chip. Even though the pin assignments are not the same for different ICs,

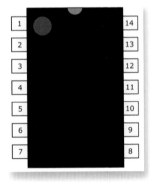

the way you determine which pin is pin 1, which is pin 2, and so on is the same for every common IC.

Here's how you figure out which pin is which for common ICs:

» Look for the *clocking mark,* which may be a small notch in the case, a little dimple in the case, or a white or colored stripe.

» Set the chip down so it looks like it's standing on its legs (pins), and orient it so that the clocking mark is on the north (12 o'clock) or northwest (11 o'clock) part of the chip.

» The upper-left pin (closest to the clocking mark) is pin 1.

» The pins are numbered counterclockwise (that is, in the reverse direction to the way in which a clock's hands move).

» The last pin (pin 8, 14, 16, or whatever) is the upper-right pin.

MEET THE 555 TIMER

The 555 timer IC is a time machine in a tiny package. This 8-pin chip can perform several timing functions, depending on how you connect it in a circuit.

I'll spare you the details of how the 555 timer works because they are technical.

This is all you need to know about the 555 timer IC for both this project and Project 6:

» **Pins 1 and 8 are used for power connections.** You connect the positive terminal of a battery to pin 8 and the negative terminal of a battery to pin 1.

» **Pins 2, 3, 4, 5, 6, and 7 are used to control what goes on inside the chip.** You connect circuit components (most often resistors or capacitors) or power levels (meaning the positive or negative side of a battery) to these pins in a certain arrangement so as to make the circuit inside the 555 timer IC operate in a particular way.

» **Pin 3 is the output pin.** Depending on what's going on inside the chip, the output pin is, in a sense, either on or off. In reality, it either has a voltage equal to the battery voltage applied to it (on) or it has no voltage applied to it (off). In electronics, the on state is known as *high* and the off state is known as *low*.

The idea is to connect something you want the chip to control, such as an LED (with a protective resistor), to the output pin. When the output pin goes high, the LED is on. When the output pin goes low, the LED is off.

In this project, you connect *two* LEDs (with protective resistors) to the output pin: One LED-resistor pair is connected between the output pin and the negative side of the battery, and the other LED-resistor pair is connected between the output pin and the positive side of the battery. With this arrangement, when the output pin goes high, one LED turns on and the other LED turns off. When the output pin goes low, the opposite happens.

The specific arrangement and values of the resistors and capacitors determine exactly when — and for how long — the output pin goes high or low. The values chosen for this project are designed to light each LED for about 1/3 of a second.

COLLECT COMPONENTS AND TOOLS

Gather all the parts in this list:

» Solderless breadboard, prepared with

 » 9-volt battery with battery clip

 » Power switch and jumper wire

 » Power rail jumper-wire connections

» One LM555 timer IC

» One 0.01 µF film (nonpolarized) capacitor

» One 4.7 µF electrolytic (polarized) capacitor

» Two 330-ohm resistors (orange-orange-brown)

» One 10-kohm resistor (brown-black-orange)

» One 100-kohm resistor (brown-black-yellow)

» Two 5 mm red LEDs

» Two 5/16-inch (minimum) jumper wires

» One 3/8-inch (minimum) jumper wire

» One 1-inch (minimum) jumper wire

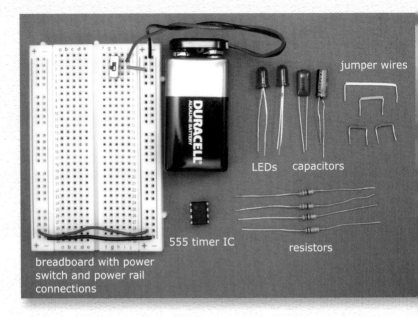

jumper wires

LEDs   capacitors

555 timer IC

resistors

breadboard with power
switch and power rail
connections

You also need your needle-nose pliers and wire cutter for this
project.

BUILD THE RAILROAD CROSSING CIRCUIT

In this project, you use a 555 timer chip to make two LEDs turn
on and off, so that when one LED is on, the other is off, and vice
versa. You control the timing of the 555 timer chip's output using
two resistors and a capacitor.

Follow these steps to build your railroad crossing circuit:

1   Double-check your solderless breadboard.

    a.   Make sure that the two positive power rails are
connected and the two negative power rails are
connected.

    b.   Check that your battery switch and jumper wire
connections are properly installed and that the switch
is in the off position.

c. Verify that the leads from your battery clip are snugly plugged into the correct contact holes in your breadboard.

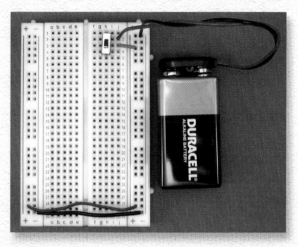

2 Insert the 555 timer chip into the breadboard.

The eight pins on this chip are sturdy, but you still have to be careful not to bend them when you insert them into the contact holes in your breadboard.

 The best way to insert an IC in a breadboard is to place the IC on top of the contact holes, gently direct its pins into the openings of the contact holes, and then press down slowly on the top of the chip to ease the pins into the holes.

a. Orient the 555 timer IC with the dimple (known as the *clocking mark*) in the upper-left corner.

 See the sidebar "Pay attention to the pinout!" to find out about the clocking mark and how the pins of an IC are numbered.

b. Place the chip on top of holes **13-16e** (left side of chip) and **13-16f** (right side of chip), so that you are lining up the corner pins like this: pin 1 into hole **13e,** pin 4 into hole **16e,** pin 5 into hole **16f,** and pin 8 into hole **13f.**

c. Press down slowly on the body of the chip, applying even pressure across the top of the chip, to insert the pins into the contact holes. As you press down, look at all the pins to make sure they are going into the holes. If any pin is not going in, stop pressing down, gently guide the pin into the hole, and then press down on the chip again until the pins are snugly inserted.

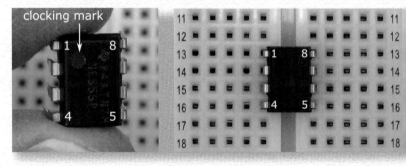

The underside of the chip should be laying right on the breadboard, and the chip should be level — not tilted right or left. If one side of the chip is tilted up, chances are the pins on that side are not properly inserted into the breadboard.

3 **Insert a 5/16-inch (minimum) jumper wire into the breadboard.**

Plug one end of the jumper wire into hole **13a** and the other end of the jumper wire into the negative power rail to the left of row **13**.

4 **Insert the 1-inch (minimum) jumper wire into the breadboard.**

This jumper wire connects pins 2 and 6 on the 555 timer IC. Plug one end of the jumper wire into hole **14d** and the other end of the jumper wire into hole **15g**.

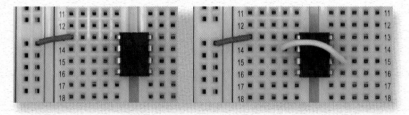

5 **Insert the 4.7 µF electrolytic capacitor into the breadboard.**

   a. Trim the capacitor leads so that each lead is about 1/2-inch long below the body of the capacitor.

   b. Plug the negative side (identified by a minus sign or black stripe) into the negative power rail on the left (I used the hole next to row 14). Plug the positive (unlabeled) side into hole **14a**.

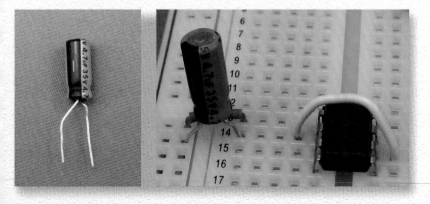

6 **Insert the two 330-ohm resistors (orange-orange-brown) into the breadboard.**

   a. Bend and trim the leads of both resistors.

   b. Plug the leads of one 330-ohm resistor into holes **11c** and **15c**.

   c. Plug the leads of the other 330-ohm resistor into holes **15d** and **19d**.

7 **Insert the 3/8-inch (minimum) jumper wire into the breadboard.**

Plug one end of the jumper wire into hole **16a** and the other end of the jumper wire into the positive power rail to the left of row **16**.

8 **Insert the 0.01 μF capacitor into the breadboard.**

   a. Bend and trim the capacitor leads so that they are about 1/2-inch long below the body of the capacitor.

   b. Plug one lead (either one) into hole **16j** and the other lead into the negative power rail to the right of row **16**.

9 **Insert the 100-kohm resistor (brown-black-yellow) into the breadboard.**

    a. Bend one of the resistor's leads so that it is parallel to the other lead.

    b. Trim both leads so that each lead extends about 1/4 inch beyond the body of the resistor.

    c. Plug one lead into hole **14h** and the other lead into hole **15h.**

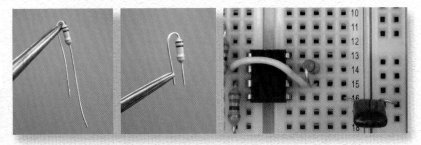

10 **Insert the 10-kohm resistor (black-brown-orange) into the breadboard.**

Bend and trim the resistor leads. Then plug the leads of the 10-kohm resistor into holes **14i** and the positive power rail to the right of row **14.**

11 **Insert a 5/16-inch (minimum) jumper wire into the breadboard.**

Plug one end of the jumper wire into hole **13j** and the other end of the jumper wire into the positive power rail to the right of row **13.**

12 Insert one of the two red LEDs into the breadboard.

Leave the LED leads untrimmed so that the LEDs stick up from your breadboard and are easy to see.

Plug the cathode (negative side, shorter lead, flat edge, large piece of metal inside the case) into hole **11a,** and the anode (positive side, longer lead, smaller piece of metal inside the case) into the positive power rail to the left of row **11.**

13 Insert the other red LED into the breadboard.

Plug the anode (positive side, longer lead, smaller piece of metal inside the case) into hole **19a** and the cathode (negative side, shorter lead, flat edge, larger piece of metal inside the case) into the negative power rail to the left of row **19.**

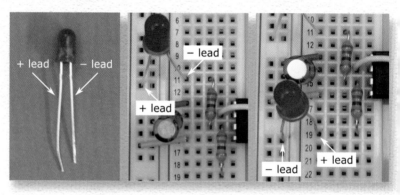

Note that the two LEDs are oriented differently in the circuit: The negative side (cathode) of the LED in row 11 is in the center section of the breadboard (in hole 11a), while the negative side of the LED in row 19 is in the negative power rail.

Double-check all your connections and the orientation of the 4.7 μF electrolytic capacitor and both of the LEDs. Once you've checked your circuit, you'll be ready to make the LEDs flash.

OPERATE THE RAILROAD CROSSING CIRCUIT

Turn on the power switch. Are the two LEDs in your circuit flashing on and off in an alternating fashion? They should be! If one or both LEDs are not flashing, check your connections again.

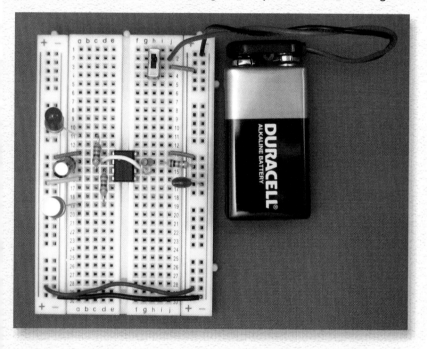

If one LED is flashing and the other isn't, check the orientation and breadboard connections of the non-flashing LED. It may be inserted backward or one of its leads may not be inserted firmly in the correct hole.

Once your railroad crossing circuit is working, try to estimate how long it takes for the LEDs to go through one full on/off cycle. It should be less than one second.

IN THIS PROJECT, YOU USE JUST SEVEN COMPONENTS, A BATTERY, AND A FLASHLIGHT (YES! A FLASHLIGHT!) TO GENERATE SOME INTERESTING SOUND EFFECTS. You can use this circuit to re-create the revving of a race car engine, a creaking door, a drum roll, the siren on a police car or firetruck, and much more.

Does this project sound like fun? If so, let's get ready to make some noise!

MINI-SPEAKER

In this project, you use a mini-speaker to play the sound effects. Speakers usually come with leads attached. The leads are twisted together to keep things neat and tidy. You attach the leads to components in your circuit so that electrical current passes from your circuit into the speaker. The speaker then converts the current into sound.

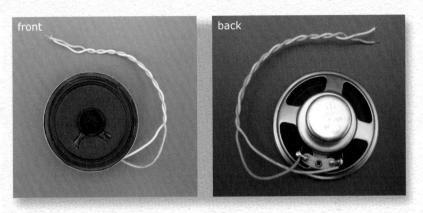

front   back

GATHER THE PARTS YOU NEED

Collect all the parts on this list:

- » Solderless breadboard, prepared with
    - » 9-volt battery with battery clip
    - » Power switch and jumper wire
    - » Power rail jumper-wire connections
- » One 8-ohm speaker, along with the following items:
    - » Two 2-inch (or so) 22-gauge solid wires with stripped ends
    - » Two insulated mini alligator clips
- » One LM555 timer IC
- » One photoresistor
- » Two 0.01 µF film (nonpolarized) capacitors
- » One 4.7 µF electrolytic (polarized) capacitor
- » One 47-kohm resistor (yellow-violet-orange)

» One 100-kohm resistor (brown-black-yellow)

» Three 5/16-inch (minimum) jumper wires

» Two 3/8-inch (minimum) jumper wires

» One 1-inch (minimum) jumper wire

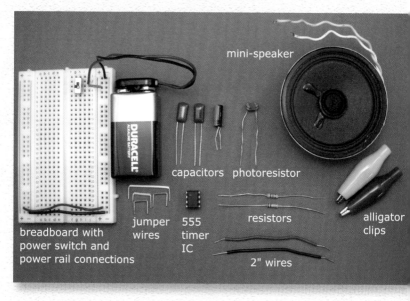

mini-speaker

capacitors   photoresistor

jumper   555   resistors   alligator
wires   timer   clips
IC

breadboard with
power switch and
power rail connections   2" wires

Have your wire cutters handy for trimming leads and your needle-nose pliers nearby for inserting components into your breadboard. And grab a flashlight (any kind) or LED camping lantern for when you operate your circuit.

PREPARE YOUR SPEAKER

Each lead wire on most speakers is made from *stranded wire,* which is a bunch of very fine wires twisted together. Stranded wire doesn't easily plug into the contact holes in a breadboard, so you need to attach solid wires to the speaker wires to use the speaker in your circuit.

If you (or a friend) know how to solder (pronounced "sodder"), you may want to solder solid wires to the speaker's lead wires. If not, simply read on for another way to attach solid wires.

It's easy to attach solid lead wires to the speaker wires without soldering. You need two jumper wires (at least 2 inches long each) and two mini alligator clips from your parts list.

An *alligator clip* is a metal fastener that resembles the jaws of a gator. The gripping part of the alligator clip contains metal teeth designed to hold wires or leads together.

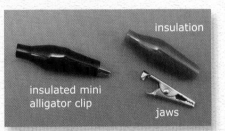

For each speaker wire, use a mini alligator clip to connect the end of the speaker wire to one end of the jumper wire, as follows:

1 **Press the separated sides of the clip together to open the jaws.**

2 **Place the end of the speaker wire and one end of the jumper wire in the jaws.**

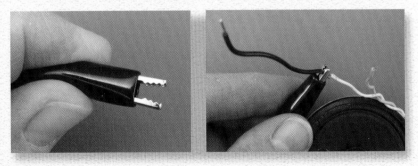

3 **Release the side of the clip that you are pressing on.**

4 **Gently tug on each wire to make sure it's secure in the jaws of the clip.**

If either or both wires come loose, repeat Steps 1–3.

The solid wire leads you attached to your speaker make it much easier to use the speaker in your breadboarded circuit.

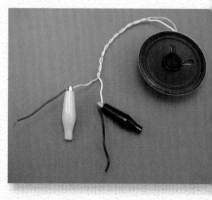

THE PLAN

For this project, you connect your speaker to the output of a 555 timer chip. The voltage at the output of the chip varies between 0 V and 9 V, depending on how you control the chip. You control the chip by connecting certain values of resistance and capacitance to some of the chip's pins.

Initially, you use resistors and capacitors with values chosen so that a single *tone*, or musical note, is played by your speaker. Let's call this circuit a *tone generator*.

Once you get your tone generator working, you swap out one of the resistors for a photoresistor, which is a light-dependent resistor. This small change results in the speaker generating different tones depending on how much light is shining on your circuit, which is now a sound effects circuit. Using a flashlight to vary the amount of light, you can then create some interesting sound effects.

Ready to get started?

BUILD THE TONE GENERATOR

Follow these steps to build your tone generator circuit:

1 **Double-check your solderless breadboard.**

   a. Make sure that the two positive power rails are connected and the two negative power rails are connected.

   b. Check that your battery switch and jumper wire connections are properly installed and that the switch is in the off position.

   c. Verify that the leads from your battery clip are snugly plugged into the correct contact holes in your breadboard.

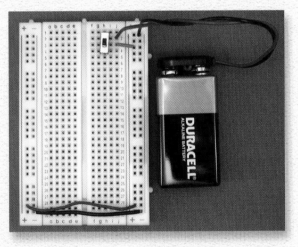

2 **Insert the 555 timer chip into the breadboard.**

   a. Orient the 555 timer IC with the dimple (clocking mark) in the upper-left corner.

   b. Place the chip on top of holes *13-16e* (left side of chip) and *13-16f* (right side of chip), so that you are lining up the corner pins like this: pin 1 into hole *13e,* pin 4 into hole *16e,* pin 5 into hole *16f,* and pin 8 into hole *13f.*

c. Press down slowly on the body of the chip until the pins are snugly inserted into the contact holes.

d. Make sure that the underside of the chip is laying flat on the breadboard surface.

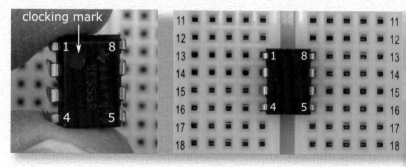

3 **Insert a 5/16-inch (minimum) jumper wire into the breadboard.**

Plug one end of the jumper wire into hole **13a** and the other end of the jumper wire into the negative power rail to the left of row **13**.

4 **Insert the 1-inch (minimum) jumper wire into the breadboard.**

This jumper wire connects pins 2 and 6 on the 555 timer IC. Plug one end of the jumper wire into hole **14d** and the other end of the jumper wire into hole **15g**.

5 **Insert one of the 0.01 µF film capacitors into the breadboard.**

a. Bend and trim the capacitor leads so that each lead is about 3/8-inch long below the bend. (You may have already trimmed the leads of a 0.01 µF capacitor for Project 5.)

b. This capacitor is nonpolarized, meaning it doesn't matter which way you orient it in a circuit. Plug one lead into hole **14a** and the other lead into the negative power rail to the left of row **14.**

6 Insert the 4.7 µF electrolytic capacitor into the breadboard.

a. Trim the capacitor leads so that each lead is about 1/2-inch long below the body of the capacitor. (You may have already trimmed the leads of a 4.7 µF capacitor for Project 5.)

b. Plug the negative side (identified by a minus sign or black stripe) into hole **19c.**

c. Plug the positive (unlabeled) side into hole **15c.**

7 Insert the 3/8-inch (minimum) jumper wire into the breadboard.

Plug one end of the jumper wire into hole **16a** and the other end of the jumper wire into the positive power rail to the left of row **16.**

8 Insert the other 0.01 µF capacitor into the breadboard.

a. Trim the capacitor leads so that they are about 1/2-inch long below the body of the capacitor.

b. Plug one lead (either one) into hole **16j** and the other lead into the negative power rail to the right of row **16.**

9 **Insert the 47-kohm resistor (yellow-violet-orange) into the breadboard.**

a. Bend one of the resistor's leads so that it is parallel to the other lead.

b. Trim both leads so that each lead extends about 1/4 inch beyond the body of the resistor.

c. Plug one lead into hole **14h** and the other lead into hole **15h.**

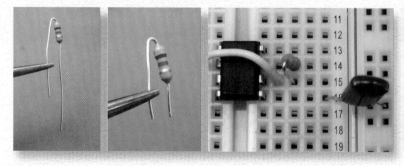

10 **Insert the 100-kohm resistor (black-brown-yellow) into the breadboard.**

Bend and trim the resistor leads. Then plug the leads of the 100-kohm resistor into holes **14i** and the positive power rail to the right of row **14.**

11 **Insert a 5/16-inch (minimum) jumper wire into the breadboard.**

Plug one end of the jumper wire into hole **13j** and the other end of the jumper wire into the positive power rail to the right of row **13.**

12 **Insert the speaker into the breadboard.**

Plug one of the leads (either one) into hole **19a** and the other lead into any hole in the negative power rail on the left. (I used the hole to the left of row **19.**)

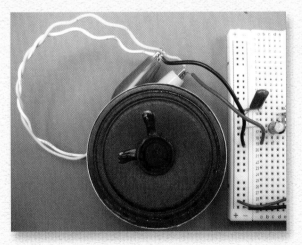

Double-check all your connections and the orientation of the 555 timer IC and the 4.7 µF electrolytic capacitor. Once you have checked your circuit, you're ready to test it.

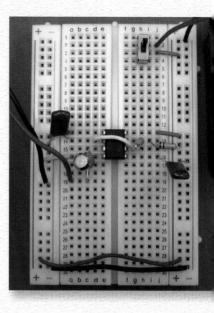

TEST YOUR TONE GENERATOR

Turn on the power switch. Do you hear a tone from the speaker? You should! If you don't hear anything, check your connections again. Still no tone? Turn off the power switch, check the orientation of the 555 timer IC, and double-check the values of the resistors and capacitors in your circuit. Then go back through the steps to build the circuit and make any necessary corrections. Replace the battery, if necessary.

Once you get your tone generator circuit working, it's time to make one small change so you can create sound effects.

MODIFY YOUR CIRCUIT

To transform your circuit from a tone generator to a sound effects generator, you simply need to replace the 100-kohm resistor with a photoresistor. Follow these steps:

1 **Turn off the power switch.**

Before you make any changes to a circuit, it's a good idea to make sure that the power is off.

2 **Remove the 100-kohm resistor (brown-black-yellow) from row 14.**

Your needle-nose pliers can help make it easier to remove the resistor.

3 **Insert a photoresistor into the breadboard.**

Plug one lead (either one) of the photoresistor into hole **14i** and the other lead into a hole in the positive power rail next to row **14.**

After you've altered your circuit, turn on your power switch. Your circuit should generate a tone or other noise. If you don't hear anything, double-check that the photoresistor is inserted firmly in the correct holes in the breadboard. If you still don't hear anything, try using another photoresistor.

CREATE SOUND EFFECTS

Once your sound effects circuit is working, you can create different sound effects by adjusting the amount of light shining on the photoresistor.

With the power switch off, turn off the room lights, close the shades, and try to make the room dark. Then turn on the power switch. Do you hear a low-pitched tone or clicking from your speaker (which might remind you of a drum roll)?

Next, grab your flashlight! Holding it behind your back, turn it on. Then, very slowly, move the flashlight from behind your back to the front of your body, closer to your circuit. Does the *pitch* (that is, how high the tone sounds) of the sound increase as you move the flashlight? Does your circuit sound a bit like a creaky door?

Now hold the flashlight behind your back again. Move the flashlight from behind your back to the front of your body, closer to your circuit, but this time move it a little bit faster than before. Does the sound remind you of the revving of a race car engine?

Next, shine the flashlight directly on the photoresistor. Is the pitch of the sound noticeably higher than when the flashlight wasn't shining directly on the photoresistor?

Hold your flashlight face down about six inches above your circuit, and then rotate your wrist to move the flashlight in a circular motion above your circuit. Is your circuit making a sound like a police siren?

Now turn on the room lights and listen to the sound from your speaker. Use your fingers to cover up the photoresistor, and then tap one or more fingers on the photoresistor (that is, move your finger on and off the photoresistor) repeatedly to create a warbling sound. To get a higher pitched sound, shine your flashlight on your circuit with the room lights on.

Experiment with different indoor light levels. Then bring your circuit outside and try it in direct sunlight, in shadowy areas, and in other places. See how many different sound effects you can make using a combination of different room lighting, flashlight positioning, and hand movements.

DO YOU ENJOY LISTENING TO THE RADIO? Would you like to build a radio of your own?

In this project, you use just one electronic component, some wire, and a few household items to build a radio receiver. Your radio receiver picks up radio signals in the air and tunes into a single radio station. When you connect your radio receiver to a special kind of earphone, you can hear the tiny radio signal.

WHAT IS RADIO?

In scientific terms, *radio* is the transmission (that is, sending) of a certain kind of electromagnetic energy through the air. *Electromagnetic energy* is energy that is *radiated*, or given off, by an object and travels in waves, similar to the way sound is transmitted. X-rays, microwaves, visible light, and ultraviolet light (think sunburn) are other types of electromagnetic energy.

One way in which X-rays, microwaves, light, and radio waves differ is in the length of their waves. Have you ever thrown a rock into a calm lake? When the rock hits the lake, the water on the surface begins to ripple, which means that little waves are created and grow in an expanding circle around the center (where the rock hit). The distance between the peaks of neighboring ripples is the *wavelength* of the ripple. Different forms of electromagnetic energy are radiated at different wavelengths, which is how we tell them apart.

The frequency of the electromagnetic energy is closely related to the wavelength. *Frequency* is a measure of how many complete cycles, or up-and-down waves, pass a given point in space each second. The longer the wavelength, the shorter the frequency, and vice versa.

Radio stations are commonly identified by their transmission frequencies, which are measured in units called hertz (abbreviated Hz). One *hertz* is one cycle per second. For instance, 1010 WINS is an AM radio station in New York City. The *1010* in its name refers to

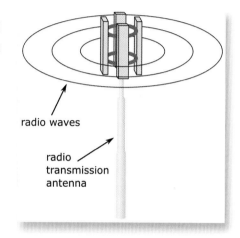

radio waves

radio transmission antenna

1010 kilohertz (kHz, which is 1000 hertz), which is the frequency at which the radio waves are transmitted from the station's antenna. Another NY-based radio station, 95.5 WPLJ, is an FM station that transmits at 95.5 megahertz (MHz, or 1 million hertz).

The radio frequency (RF) spectrum (that is, range of frequencies) is used for TV, short wave, cellphone, GPS, and other types of transmissions in addition to radio station transmissions. Each AM radio station transmits at a frequency between 535 kHz and 1700 kHz, and

(continued)

(continued)

each FM radio station transmits at a frequency between 87.5 MHz and 108 MHz.

Radio transmitters send *information*, which can be music or speech, over RF waves by modifying the pattern of the RF waves in a way that is related to the electrical pattern, or *signal*, representing the music or speech. This process is known as *modulation*. The RF waves are *carriers* of the actual signal (for instance, music). At the receiving end, a radio receiver *demodulates* the RF waves, separating the signal from the carrier. The signal can then be amplified by an electronic circuit and played through a speaker or headphones.

Although this radio transmission and reception process sounds complicated, building a basic radio receiver is actually simple.

PLAN YOUR MISSION

Your job in this project is to pull a single radio signal, or frequency, out of the air and send it to an earphone so you can hear it. Sounds simple enough, doesn't it? As long as there is at least one reasonably strong AM radio station near your location, you should be able to detect a radio signal.

If you live in an area that is far from an AM radio station, you may not be able to detect a radio signal. But it's worth a try to see if you can.

To pull a single radio signal out of the air, you need

» An *antenna* to collect all the electromagnetic energy from the air. The antenna you use in this project is a long wire connected to a large metal object, such as a coffee can.

» A *tuner* to select just one radio frequency. Your tuner consists of an *inductor* (a coil of wire) and a *variable capacitor* (a capacitor that can be adjusted to store different amounts of electric charge). In the next sections, you find out how to make your own inductor and variable capacitor.

» A radio wave *detector* to pull the signal (music or speech) from the tuned signal. Your detector is a specific kind of diode made from germanium.

Then, to hear the signal, you need a special type of earphone that is sensitive enough to transform the weak signal coming out of your radio wave detector into sound.

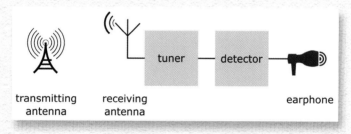

transmitting antenna   receiving antenna   tuner   detector   earphone

HOMEMADE TUNER

You can make your own tuner by using several household items along with a special kind of wire (which you purchase in a store or online). In this section, you find out how to make your own inductor and variable capacitor. These parts work together to tune in a specific radio frequency.

Here are the supplies you need:

» A spool of 24-gauge magnet wire (50 feet minimum)

Magnet wire is copper wire with a very thin enamel coating that serves as insulation. Don't be fooled by the appearance of magnet wire; it is not bare copper wire, even though it looks as shiny as metal.

» Two 12-inch jumper wires

» One empty toilet paper (TP) roll, free of all paper and glue

» One empty paper towel roll, free of all paper and glue

» One small piece of medium or coarse (40 to 80 grit) sandpaper

» Aluminum foil

» One plain white sheet of paper (such as printer paper)

» Transparent tape (the kind you use to wrap gifts) or masking tape

MAKE AN INDUCTOR

All you need to make your own inductor is the TP roll, magnet wire, sandpaper, some tape — and a lot of patience.

Follow these steps to make your inductor:

1 **Starting about 1 inch from one end of the TP roll, use your thumb to hold the magnet wire against the TP roll, leaving about 10 inches of magnet wire free.**

2 **Wind the magnet wire around the roll, holding it in place with your thumb and counting the number of turns.**

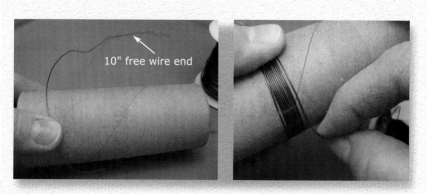

10" free wire end

TIP

Make sure that each turn of the wire lies flat against the TP roll and is as close as possible to the previous turns. Avoid kinking the wire or overlapping turns.

3 When you've wound 5 to 10 turns of wire, you may want to use some tape to secure the wire in place against the TP roll.

4 Continue to wind the wire until you've counted 100 turns.

TIP

You may need to periodically adjust the wire to ensure that the turns are wound close together without any overlap or kinks.

5 Use tape to hold the 100 turns of wire in place against the TP roll.

6 **Cut the end of the wire about 10 inches after the last turn.**

You should have about 10 inches of free wire on each end of the 100 turns.

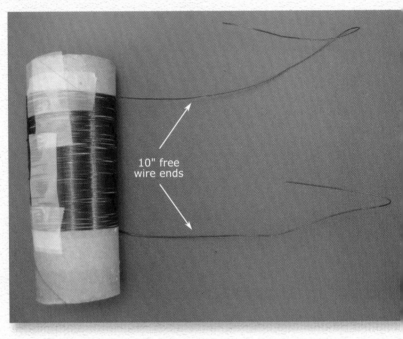

10" free wire ends

7 **Sand about 1 inch of the enamel coating off each of the two ends of your coil.**

Fold your sandpaper over one end of the wire and move the sandpaper back and forth, squeezing it against the wire, until the copper underneath the enamel is exposed. Repeat the sanding process for the other end of the wire.

folded sandpaper

1"

bare copper

enamel coating

Exposing the copper core at each end of the wire enables you to connect your inductor to your circuit. Leaving the enamel on the rest of the wire prevents the individual turns of the wire from making electrical contact with each other.

This simple coil of wire plays an important part in tuning your radio.

MAKE A VARIABLE CAPACITOR

The other component of your homemade radio tuner is a variable capacitor. Grab the paper towel roll, aluminum foil, paper, two 12-inch jumper wires, and tape. Then follow these steps to make your variable capacitor:

1 **Carefully cut two pieces of aluminum foil roughly 5 1/2 inches by 6 1/2 inches each.**

The foil should be as smooth as possible.

2 **Tape the 5 1/2-inch side of one piece of foil to one end of the paper towel roll.**

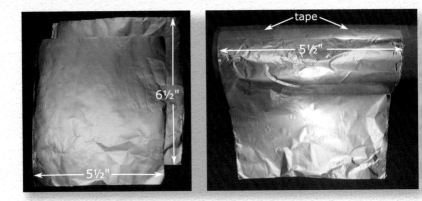

3 **Wrap the foil around the paper towel roll and tape the free end down.**

Smooth the foil as you wrap it. The two ends should overlap.

tape the overlapping foil down

4 **Cut a piece of plain paper 5 3/4 by 6 inches.**

5 **Lay the second piece of foil on top of the paper as follows:**

  a. On three sides, make sure that the paper is visible under the foil.

  b. On the fourth side, make sure that the foil hangs over the edge of the paper by about 1/2 inch.

  c. Tape the foil to the paper on three sides.

d. Make sure that one end of the foil sticks out over the edge of the paper.

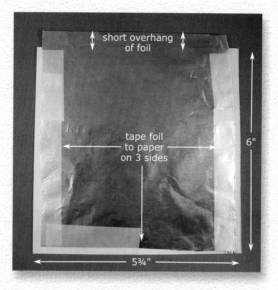

short overhang of foil

tape foil to paper on 3 sides

6"

5¾"

6 Wrap the foil-paper combination around the paper towel roll.

a. Do not tape the foil-paper combination to the paper towel roll. Instead, wrap the foil-paper combination around the paper towel roll so that it overlaps the inner foil.

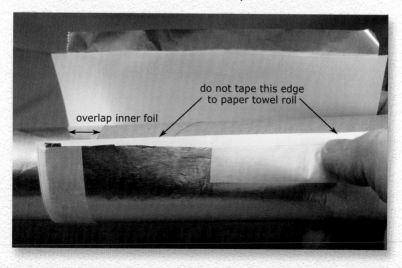

overlap inner foil

do not tape this edge to paper towel roll

b. Leave the foil-paper combination a little loose so that you can slide it up and down along the length of the paper towel roll.

c. Tape the overhanging foil edge down.

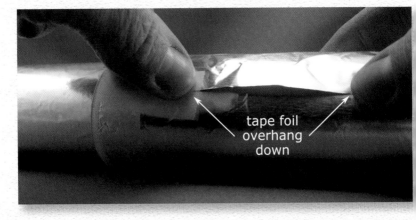

tape foil
overhang
down

Make sure you can slide the foil-paper combination up and down, but be careful to avoid sliding it too far. If it slides beyond the inner foil, you might tear the inner foil when you slide the foil-paper combination the other way. The two layers of foil should always overlap at least a little.

7 **Attach jumper wires to the two ends of the variable capacitor.**

a. Tape the stripped end of a 12-inch jumper wire to one end of the capacitor, so the bare wire makes contact with the foil.

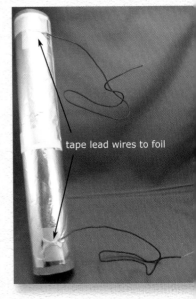

tape lead wires to foil

b. Tape the stripped end of another 12-inch jumper wire to the other end of the capacitor.

Together, your inductor and your variable capacitor will play the role of the tuner in your radio circuit.

MEET YOUR RADIO SIGNAL DETECTOR

The only electronic component you need for your radio receiver is a 1N34A germanium diode. This diode serves as the detector in your radio receiver. It separates the radio signal (which carries the important music or speech information) from the radio carrier waves.

Like all diodes, the 1N34A allows current to flow in just one direction (from anode to cathode) and needs a certain amount of voltage applied to it to conduct current. Because it is made

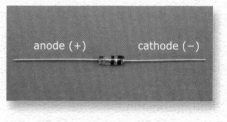

anode (+)   cathode (−)

of germanium, it needs only a tiny voltage to get it to conduct current — and that's a good thing because your radio receiver circuit doesn't have a battery! The only power source in your circuit is the power of the radio waves themselves.

CHECK OUT YOUR EARPHONE

To hear the radio signal picked up by your radio receiver, you need a piezoelectric (pronounced "pee-AY-zoh-eh-LECK-trick") earphone. Also known as a crystal earphone, a piezoelectric earphone is sensitive enough to respond to a very weak electrical signal.

To connect your earphone to your radio receiver, you need bare wire at the end of the earphone leads. If your piezoelectric earphone has a plug attached to its leads, use your wire stripper/cutter to cut the plug and strip about 1/2 inch of insulation from the end of each of the two leads.

COLLECT PARTS AND TOOLS

The variable capacitor and inductor you built in the "Homemade Tuner" section are two of the key components of your radio receiver. In addition to those homemade parts, gather the following supplies:

» One 1N34A germanium diode

» One piezoelectric earphone

» One piece of cardboard (6 inches by 6 inches or larger) or the plastic lid of a large coffee can (6 inch or larger diameter)

» Three paper fasteners (any size)

» Two long (roughly 5 feet) wires with stripped ends

» Two alligator clips

» One large metal object, such as a coffee can

» Liquid or spray glue

» Needle-nose pliers

» Optional: scissors or wire cutter

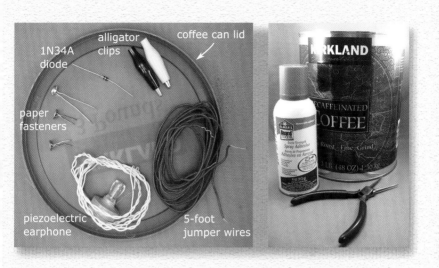

1N34A diode

alligator clips

coffee can lid

paper fasteners

piezoelectric earphone

5-foot jumper wires

WORK CLOSE TO THE (EARTH) GROUND

For your radio receiver to work, you need to make an electrical connection between your circuit and the earth. By *earth*, I mean the actual dirt in the ground outside your home. That type of connection is called an *earth ground* connection. But don't worry. You don't need to run a wire from your circuit, out a door or window, maybe down one or more flights of stairs, and all the way to the ground (although you can if you want to).

Fortunately, certain objects inside your house or apartment — such as metal radiators, metal faucets, and copper pipes — are electrically connected to the ground outside your home. Such objects serve as earth ground connections.

To connect your circuit to earth ground, you should plan to build your circuit within 5 feet or so of an earth ground connection. My circuit-building space is in an unfinished room in my basement. Copper pipes run across the ceiling in this room, with copper brackets holding the copper pipes in place. It's easy for me to attach an alligator clip to one of the copper brackets, and then use the clip to connect a wire to my circuit.

An alternative work space is my kitchen table, which is located next to a metal baseboard radiator. By removing the painted radiator cover, I can access the bare metal fins of the radiator, to which I can attach an alligator clip and make a good connection to earth ground.

PREPARE A RADIO PLATFORM

Before you connect the parts of your radio receiver, you need to create a surface on which to build the radio. Use the piece of cardboard or the plastic lid of a large coffee can and the three paper fasteners from your parts list, along with your needle-nose pliers.

Follow these steps to prepare your platform:

1 **Poke three holes in your cardboard or plastic surface.**

Use your needle-nose pliers to poke holes near the edge of your surface. Space the holes about 1 inch apart.

2 **Push the paper fasteners through the holes in your surface.**

Make sure that the flat top of each paper fastener is on the top of your surface, and flatten the two fins of each fastener against the bottom of your surface. Neighboring paper fasteners must not touch each other.

If your paper fasteners are too long (as was one of mine), you can use your scissors or wire cutter to cut them down.

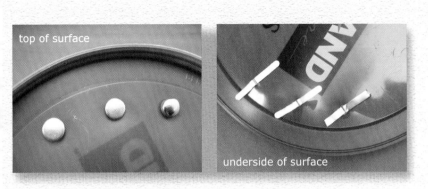

top of surface

underside of surface

BUILD THE RADIO

Your radio receiver consists of your homemade inductor, your homemade variable capacitor, the 1N34A germanium diode, a 5-foot wire antenna, and a 5-foot wire connection to earth ground. You also need two alligator clips to help make connections. Wiring these components is somewhat challenging, but if you are careful and an AM transmitter is within range, you should be able to hear the signal.

Follow these steps to build your radio:

1 Attach the 1N34A germanium diode to your radio platform.

Wrap the cathode (black striped side) lead around the middle paper fastener and wrap the anode (unmarked side) lead around one of the outer paper fasteners.

Use your needle-nose pliers to wrap each lead around each fastener, and make sure each lead is secured against its fastener.

2 Attach the variable capacitor to the radio platform:

a. Pick a spot to place the variable capacitor on your platform, leaving room for the inductor.

b. Spread or spray glue onto the area of the platform where you want to place the variable capacitor.

c. Stick the paper towel roll onto the glue so that the movable foil-paper combo is toward the top end of the paper towel roll.

d. Hold the variable capacitor against the platform for a minute or so until the glue dries.

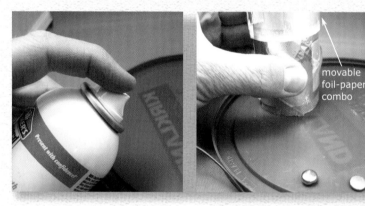

movable foil-paper combo

3 Attach the inductor to the radio platform:

a. Pick a spot to place the inductor on your platform.

b. Spread or spray glue onto the area of the platform where you want to place the inductor.

c. Stick one end (either one) of the TP roll onto the glue.

d. Hold the inductor against the platform for a minute or so until the glue dries.

4 **Connect the variable capacitor leads to the inductor leads:**

a. Hold one lead from the variable capacitor and one lead from the inductor.

b. Use your fingers to twist the bare ends of the leads together.

c. Repeat Steps 4a and 4b for the other two leads (one from the variable capacitor and one from the inductor).

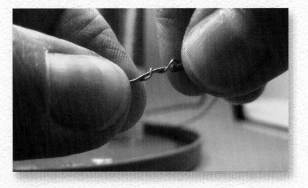

5 **Connect the two pairs of twisted leads to the outer paper fasteners:**

a. Connect one pair of twisted leads to either one of the outer paper fasteners.

b. Connect the other pair of twisted leads to the other outer paper fastener.

6 **Connect the piezoelectric earphone to two of the paper fasteners:**

a. Connect one lead (either one) to the middle paper fastener.

b. Connect the other lead to the outer paper fastener that is **not** connected to the 1N34A germanium diode.

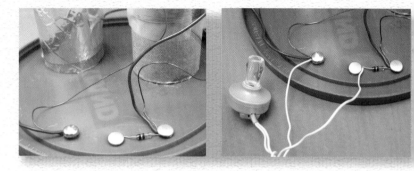

7 Connect your circuit to earth ground:

a. Use a long (at least 5-foot) wire with 1/2 inch to 1 inch of insulation stripped off each end.

b. Connect one (stripped) end of the long wire to the outer paper fastener that is **not** connected to the diode.

c. Attach the other one end to a copper pipe, metal faucet, or metal radiator fin in your house, using an alligator clip to hold the wire in place.

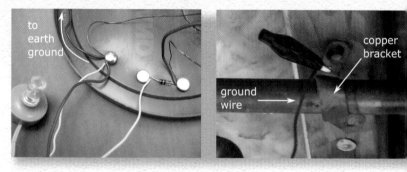

8 Connect an antenna to your circuit:

a. Attach one stripped end of a 5-foot (or longer) wire onto the outer paper fastener that is also connected to the diode.

b. Use an alligator clip to connect the other end to a large metal object (but not an object connected to earth ground). I used a large metal coffee can. The spokes of a bicycle, a large disposable aluminum pan, or an unplugged metal lamp are other possibilities.

c. Place the metal object so that the antenna is stretched out (but not tight).

Your homemade radio is done! Now it's time to check all your connections thoroughly. Once you have checked everything, you will be ready to listen to your radio.

LISTEN TO YOUR RADIO

Place the earphone in your ear. If you don't hear anything, try adjusting your variable capacitor by sliding the movable foil-paper combination up and down along the length of the paper towel roll.

Be careful not to slide the foil-paper combination too far, or you may rip the underlying foil.

If a strong enough AM radio signal is in your area, you should be able to tune it in.

If you still don't get a signal, try following these steps:

1 **Remove the earphone from your ear.**

2 **Unclip the far end of the antenna from the large metal object you attached it to in Step 8b when you built your radio.**

3 **Use your fingers on one hand to hold onto the far end of the antenna and extend your hand out.**

4 **Place the earphone back in your ear.**

5 **Hold your other arm out but don't touch anything with your second hand.**

Your body will act like an extension of the antenna, and may be enough to pull in a radio signal.

If you get a signal, try adjusting your variable capacitor to see if you can pick up another radio station. I heard two AM stations, but I live near a big city, so there are lots of stations in my area.

No luck? Check all your connections again, including the wires taped to the variable capacitor. Make sure all the wires connected to each paper fastener are making contact with each other. If you still don't hear anything, you may want to try your radio in another location that is closer to an AM radio station.

DEDICATION

To my dad, James J. Corbett, who encouraged me to pursue my interest in electrical engineering.

ABOUT THE AUTHOR

Cathleen Shamieh built her first circuit as part of a sixth-grade science fair project and knew right away that she wanted to become an engineer. She studied electrical engineering at Manhattan College and MIT, and worked for many years in the fields of medical electronics, speech processing, and telecommunications. She now works as a freelance researcher and high-tech writer.

AUTHOR'S ACKNOWLEDGMENTS

I'm grateful to have had the opportunity to work on a third book with the delightful Susan Pink, who once again played the dual roles of project and copy editor. Susan managed the process and improved upon my writing with her usual balance of grace, humor, and encouragement.

Special thanks to proofreader Debbye Butler for saving me — a former eighth-grade spelling champion — from embarrassing myself on more than one occasion. I'm also grateful to Katie Mohr for asking me to write another electronics book and to Production Editor Selvakumaran Rajendiran and the entire Wiley team for working so hard to create this book.

Thanks to my husband, Bill, and my sons, Kevin, Peter, Brendan, and Patrick, for their love and support. And, finally, a special shout out to Patrick for agreeing to appear in the radio picture at the beginning of Project 7.

PUBLISHER'S ACKNOWLEDGMENTS

Acquisitions Editor: Katie Mohr

Project and Copy Editor: Susan Pink

Production Editor: Selvakumaran Rajendiran